Cognitive Idealization

Cognitive Idealization

On the Nature and Utility of Cognitive Ideals

by

Nicholas Rescher
University Professor of Philosophy
University of Pittsburgh

Cambridge Scholars Press Ltd.
London

Cognitive Idealization: On the Nature and Utility of Cognitive Ideals
by Nicholas Rescher.

This book first published 2003 by

Cambridge Scholars Press

119 Station Road, Amersham, Buckinghamshire, HP7 0AH UK
21 Desaumarez Street, Kensington Park, South Australia 5068, Australia

British Library Cataloguing in Publication Data
A catalogue record for this book is available from the British Library

ISBN 1904303242

For Jude Dougherty
(in cordial friendship)

CONTENTS

PREFACE

Ethical idealization pivots on idealities in the sphere of human action. Cognitive idealization, by contrast, pivots on idealization in the sphere of our knowledge. Accordingly, the task of the present book is to consider the role of idealization in cognitive matters and to establish its utility in this realm. For the somewhat ironic fact of the matter is that our recourse to unrealizable idealities finds its explanation and justification in the substantial benefits that flow from such a proceeding. It is, ironically, in its utility that the rationale of ideality is to be sought.

The book brings together lines of thought about the kinship between idealism and pragmatism that have occupied my work for many years. It was conceived in 2000, produced in 2001, and polished in 2002. I am very grateful to Estelle Burris for her help in facilitating the transition from my pen into print.

Nicholas Rescher
Pittsburgh, PA
September 2002

CHAPTER ONE

IDEALS AND IDEALIZATION

I. Ideals

In the sense of the term that will be at issue here, an *ideal* represents an "idealized" view of things—a hyperbolic *image* of sorts, a mind's-eye picture of a utopian condition of affairs in which the realization of certain values is fulfilled and completed to reach "the height of imaginable perfection," as Rudolf Eisler's philosophical dictionary puts it.[1] Ideals as such are never encountered in reality but are products of the imagination and instruments for the mind. They are thought-creatures—representations of how matters should ideally stand in some respect or other. And they are fundamentally value oriented, abrogating "by hypothesis" certain limitations the real world imposes on the realization of some aspect of value. Ideals serve as our index not of what *is* or *will* be, nor just of what *can* be, but even of what *should* be. They represent a vision as to how things would stand if the complex realities of an imperfect reality did not stand in the way. For example, the ideal of human bodies (masculine and feminine) of the Greek sculptors or that of plants and animals as represented by 19th century naturalist illustrators is nowhere to be encountered in nature as we actually have it.

The employment of *ideal* as a noun is relatively recent. Lessing informs us that it was first so used by the Italian Jesuit Francesco Lana (d. 1687).[2] However, the adjective *ideal* is older; we find it (as *idealis*) in use by Albert the Great (d. 1390),[3] and by later scholastics.[4] It is clearly related to one sense of the word *idea*—namely, its Platonic sense as an idealized exemplar (*paradeigmon*, that is, *idea prima* = *examplar primum seu archetypon* as one early philosophical lexicographer put it[5]).

The modern conception of an "ideal" was disseminated through the philosophy of Kant, who wrote:

> But what I call the *ideal* seems even further removed from objective reality than the idea. By ideal I understand the idea not

merely *in concreto* but also *in individuo*, as an individual thing
determinable or even determined by the idea alone . . . The ideal
is therefore the archetype (*Urbild, prototypon*) of all things [of a
given sort], all of which, as imperfect copies (*ectypa*) derive from
it the substance of their possibility, and while approximating to it
more or less, always fall infinitely short of actually attaining it.[6]

Three points thus come together in this Kantian conception of something ideal:

(1) being paradigmatic or archetypal
(2) being complete, perfect and altogether flawless
(3) being unreal, imaginary, unrealized and indeed unrealizable as
    such but accessible in idea alone

As point (2) emphasizes, the factor of worth and value is a crucial
component of the conception of the ideal. Ideals envision a condition
of affairs in which some sort of value is realized in limitless and thus
"unrealistic" degree. The trio "liberty, equality, fraternity," which
constituted political ideals for the ideologues of the French Revolu-
tion, illustrates this circumstance. Their devotees looked to a new
order, where men, freed from the restrictive fetters of the ancient regime, would work together in cheerful cooperation for the common
good. Hoping to overcome the deficiencies of the old regime, they
envisioned the transformation to a perfected political order that neither did nor could find accommodation amid the harsh realities of an
imperfect world.

The expression "ideally speaking" indicates a completeness without let or hindrance—a perfection that goes beyond anything actually
realizable in this imperfect, sublunary dispensation. An ideal is a
model or pattern of things too perfect for actual realization in this
world. In this way, "ideally speaking" standardly contrasts with
"speaking in the ordinary common-place way." According to Cicero's
De republica, Scipio affirmed that "though others may be called men,
only those are truly men who are perfected in the arts appropriate to
humanity."[7] It is just this sort of contrast between the *real* and the
ideal that is the basis of the idea of ideals.

But of course any such realization or exemplification of an ideal
is, to some extent a travesty, something which, in going beyond reality, is also unfaithful to it. For reality inevitably introduces detail that
is uncalled for and irrelevant as far as ideas are concerned. Nothing
real ever actually captures an ideal: it inevitably encompasses details
that are, from the angle of the ideal order, little better than flaws and
imperfections. In leaving all this sort of thing out of sight, ideals fail
to accommodate reality's insistence on being presented, like Oliver

Cromwell, "with the warts on." In projecting ideals we look to something which—realistically speaking—the world cannot actually give us. We indulge in asking for something that we cannot—and do not really expect—ever actually to obtain.

Ideals are generally particularized in some way—to a profession or craft, to a particular culture or nation ("the Roman ideal of citizenship"), and in principle even to a small group (a family) or perhaps even a single person (think of Sigmund Freud's "ego-ideal" and the whole issue of the sort of person we should ideally like to be—to try to make of ourselves).

There are, of course, very different types of ideals—personal, moral, political, social, religious, cognitive, aesthetic, and others. A taxonomy of ideals would be complicated indeed, seeing that there are bound to be as many different kinds of ideals as there are kinds of values. Even "purely theoretical" issues can have their ideal aspect, as is attested by the cognitive ideal of "perfected science"—a body of knowledge capable of answering our question about nature in a way that satisfies such abstract desiderata as truth, comprehensiveness, coherence, elegance, and the other characteristic features of "the systemic ideal."

If something is my ideal, I would certainly *welcome* others also seeing it in this light. But I cannot appropriately expect or demand it. Ideals lack the sort of universality we attribute to norms; there is something more particularized, more *parochial* about them. (The Greek and the Christian ideal of man differ significantly.)

The matter of *which* particular ideal people adopt admits of variation. Ideals, like goals, are relative to the particular values to which an agent subscribes, and to the priorities he gives them; they are not inherent in his status as a rational agent *per se*. A person who subscribes to certain ideals accordingly has no right to expect that others will do so as well, though he certainly does have a right to expect that they should respect his position.

Human goods are diverse. Different people with different personal experiences and dispositions have different priorities among values. And these can be incompatible. Your ideal state may emphasize liberty, mine order; your ideal lifestyle may require ongoing novelty, mine stability and regularity. Different people will have conflicting ideals. The ideal of a world-order where everyone's ideals can be accommodated is itself an ideal—and an emphatically unrealistic one at that.

People, of course, differ in their attachment to ideals—even as they differ in their attachment to other people, to material possessions, or to anything else. Some of us are pedestrians, inextricably engaged in the quotidian round of everyday concerns; others are high-flying visionaries, given to dreaming and scheming for a better day. Some are "realists" and view the human condition with contempt; others are "persons of high ideals," devoted to visions of the good, dedicated to a better condition of things, and given to expecting much—perhaps too much—of themselves and other poor people. But *this* sort of "realism/idealism" is a matter of mixture and proportion.

II. Idealization

Idealization consists in envisioning an item of such a sort under the supposition that it plays some desired and valued role at issue completely and perfectly without any limitation whatsoever: "a perfect vacation" or "a definitive scientific theory." The item at issue, the "ideal," is to be a perfect, complete, definitive instance of its type—a very model or paradigm that answers to the purposes at issue in a way that is flawless and incapable of being improved upon: "the true friend," "the flawless performer," "the consummate physician." Such ideals, of course, are by their very nature "too good to be true."

This aspect of "idealization" attaches to all ideals. It has important consequences, because it means that we cannot expect to meet with the realization of ideals in actual experience. The *object* at issue with an ideal (perfect democracy, definitive science, full realization of our own potential, etc.) cannot be brought to completed actualization in this world. Ideals are merely visions of things about which there is always an element of the visionary. In its very nature, "ideal" provides a *contrast* to "real": there is always some tincture of the imaginary about our ideals. They are not objects we encounter in the world; it is only through thought, and specifically through the *imagination*, that we gain access to the ideal.

In interpreting an ideal as such, we have to engage in abstraction—to prescind by intellectual fiat from the complexities and imperfections that this world's realities incredibly manifest.

The traditional approach to idealization—let us call it "Platonic"—regards ideals in descriptive terms. Here we have not only Plato's *ideas* and Max Weber's "ideal types" but also such utopian variations as the ideal prince of traditional kingship literature or the ideal state of the political tradition. Kant's "regulative ideals" that serve as guides for praxis (systemic unity for inquiry, for example, or impersonal generalizability for morality) also fall into this category.

This sort of idealization also figures in the characterization of organizational structures, as when one spells out the "job description" for various functionaries: the superintendent, the service department head, the chief engineer, etc. Here we do not deal with concrete human beings in their full blown idiosyncratic personhood but see them simply as generic functionaries benefit of all human particularity. What we thus confront in real life is always something very different—the womanizing director, say, or the alcoholic chief accountant.

Throughout this sort of idealization we engage in an abstraction from the sort of detail that is inescapable with the membership of the real-world. In comparison to the furnishings of the real world those idealizations are incomplete, schematic, "abstract."

Take something as simple as a play—Shakespeare's *Hamlet*, say. As such it is an abstraction, a schematic and descriptively incomplete pattern that can be fleshed out in a performance by actors who (unlike Hamlet in abstract) must speak in a particular tone of voice and bear a particular number of hairs on their heads. And no matter how elaborate the stage directors may be, the gap can never be closed by filling in every detail: every breath drawn, every instruction, ever gesture and movement, etc. To concretize any such abstraction requires more than one could ever abstractly indicate—it requires the detail of a performative interpretation.

To be sure, on must accordingly distinguish between full-scale ideals and mini-ideals, between (1) something that is altogether and unqualifiedly perfect, and (2) something that is "as perfect as we can realistically expect to find," or "as perfect as is requisite for the immediate purpose at hand." It is the second, rather than the first, that is at issue in locutions like

- "That hammer is the ideal tool for the job."
- "She was an ideal wife for him."
- "Florida was an ideal locale for our midwinter vacation."

It is not this latter, qualified sort of ideality but the former, unqualified sort that will concern us here.

When we "idealize" is this stronger sense, we begin by considering some valued type of thing or state of affairs, characterized in functional, use- or role-oriented terms of being good *for* something. For example:

- a vacation: a period of time spent away from one's ordinary duties and dedicated to rest and relaxation
- a scientific theory: a thesis or hypothesis used to provide an explanatory account for some entity or process in nature

Idealization consists in envisioning an item of such a sort under the supposition that it plays the valued role at issue completely and perfectly without any limitations whatsoever: "a perfect vacation" of "a definitive scientific theory." The item at issue, the "ideal," is to be a perfect, complete, definitive instance of its type—a very model or paradigm that answers to the purposes at issue in a way that is flawless and incapable of being improved upon: "the true friend," "the flawless performer," "the consummate physician." Such ideals, of course, are "too good to be true."

We must accordingly reckon with the unrealism of our ideals. The ardent socialist who adopts economic equality as one of his ideal need not (and should not) expect it to be realized in full. He doubtless cannot even say just precisely what its concrete realization would actually be like. (For example, even if X and Y were fitted out with the same "goods and possessions," how could one make provision for their different tastes, needs, and capacities for enjoyment?) Again, suppose I were an ardent capitalist, who adopted free and unfettered competition as one of my cardinal ideals. The awkward fact remains that the production of some major goods, such as "public health" or "national security," just does not square with this model. There is something unrealistic about our ideals: they are inherently incapable of "genuine fulfillment."

III. The Orienting Role of Ideals: Ideals as Useful Fictions

Ideals are in a way akin to such quasi-fictive reference devices as the equator or the prime meridian, which we do not actually encounter in physical embodiment on the world's stage. They are "navigation aids" as it were—thought constructions that we superimpose on the messy realities of this world to help us find our way about. It is not their reality but their utility that constitutes the crux for the legitimation of an ideal, and their utility of an ideal lies in its capacity to guide evaluation and to direct action in productive ways. Ideals' crucial role is as a tool for intelligent planning of the conduct of life. To manage our own affairs satisfactorily—and to explain and understand how others manage theirs—we must exploit the guiding power of ideals.

For this reason, philosophers concerned with the elucidation of human goods and values find an idealization a particularly useful device. Time and again we see them resorting to such idealizations as

- the perfectly just man of Plato
- the perfectly wise man of the Stoics
- the ideal community of utopian political theorizing
- the social contract between ideally rational agents

- the perfection of inquiry in "ideal science" (Kant, Peirce)
- the "perfectly rational agent" of economic theorizing

In all such cases, we are confronted by an idealization invoked to explain and validate some major project of human endeavor.

Many of our key concepts about types of things are idealizations through being predicated on a normative/evaluative conception that looks to an ideal in that the normative characterizations involved have to be construed with a certain element of idealization in view. Typical instances of the sort of thing at issue here are such traditional philosophical centerpiece as the true, the good, the just, the desirable.

- The *fully true* statement is one that completely realizes all the desiderata that a communicatively appropriate statement ought ideally to realize: it presents not just nothing but the truth of the matter but all of the relevant truth.
- A *truly just* action or decision is one that achieves the desiderata than morally appropriate action or decision ought ideally to realize.
- A *totally fair* exchange is one that realizes the conditions a rationally designed exchange aught ideally to realize.
- A *desirable* thing or state of affairs is one that achieves that which an appropriate arrangement ought ideally to be realized.
- A *perfect X* (gentleman, automobile, banana) is an X that realizes the conditions that an X ought ideally to realize.

In this sort of way, such desiderata as the True, the Just, the Desirable, etc. has to be defined or specified with a view to a state of idealization. All ideas of this sort are inherently ideality-purporting: they represent concepts that take their place against the backdrop of the projection of a certain particular mode of ideality. They are defined with reference to an ideal. After all, if a statement is not perfectly (fully, absolutely, totally, completely) true then it just isn't *true*—"almost true," or "merely true," or "approximately true" maybe, but not flat-out true. And the same with the totally just or the altogether desirable.

We do not expect to attain the ideal, since we recognize full well that an impassable barrier separates us from its actualization. But, miragelike, it beckons us onward. It does two things for us: (1) it does not let us rest content with simply staying where we are, and, still more importantly, (2) it furnishes us with guidance by orienting us with the guiding vision (however visionary!) of a better order of things. Preventing us from resting comfortably content with what it is we actually achieve, ideals lure us on, Siren-fashion, toward a better order of things—an order we are drawn to pursue unless we firmly bind ourselves, with Ulysses as precedent, to the mast of the world's realities. (Bitter experience tend to do this for us, which is why the old are generally less idealistic than the young.)

By providing such bases of judgment, ideals serve to orient and structure our action-guiding thought and give meaning and significance to our endeavors. They are guiding beacons across the landscape of life—distant, even unreachable points of reference that help us to find our way. We frequently should, generally can, and sometimes actually do design our own courses of action and evaluate those of others by using ideals as a reference standard.

To adopt an ideal is emphatically not to think its realization to be possible. Even when we cultivate or pursue an ideal we do (or should!) recognize from the start that it lies beyond the reach of practical attainability. Ideals accordingly do not constitute the concrete objectives of our practical endeavors but rather provide them with some generalized direction. Moreover, objectives are simply things we want and desire—for *whatever* reason. There is no suggestion that they are inherently valuable or worthy. But by their very nature ideals are held by their exponents to be objects of worth. An ideal of mine is not just something I want; it is a condition I am committed to considering as deserving of being sought. By their very nature, ideals are seen not as mere objects of desire (*desideranda*): what counts with them is not what one finds that people do want but what one judges to be worthy of wanting.

Ideals also differ importantly from norms. Take morality, for example. A moral norm specifies what *must* (or *must not*) be if violence to the moral order is to be avoided—i.e., if the *minimal* demands of morality are to be instituted in the human community. A moral ideal, on the other hand, specifies positively what *should* be if the moral order is to be perfected in a given direction—i.e., if certain *maximal* demands of morality are to be instituted. In the moral sphere ideals reach out beyond norms, beyond the *via negativa* prohibitions of those "thou shalt not" commandments, toward the ampler demands of a utopian order of things. Thus moral ideals do not abrogate norms but extend or amplify them.

Our practical endeavors must ultimately be guided by the vision of an end beyond the practical range. Behind the "letter of the law" there must be a "spirit of the law." Rules and reasons cannot prevail everywhere, at every successive stage of the justificatory process. Eventually their guidance runs out of steam, and such further guidance as we require must come from the illumination of an ideal. To stick with rules and reasons always and everywhere is actually inhumane. Their operation must function in a setting where there is some room for appeal "beyond the rules"—be it from commiseration, sympathy, kindness, or whatever—to some tempering influence from an idealized vision of human life. It is, after all, this sort of guiding vision that provides the rationale for the rules in the first place.

Having *some* degree of involvement with values and ideals is part and parcel of being a normal human being. Man is an amphibious creature, constrained by the circumstances of his condition to operate in two realms, the real and the ideal—the domain of what is and the domain of what ought to be.

IV. Obstacles to Idealization

All ideals involve the element of *idealization*. They represent putative aspects of excellence considered in isolation apart from other aspects. When we consider such values in separation from others, we engage in an act of *abstraction*—we put all other considerations aside for the time being. This, of course, is ultimately untenable—and so we have here another aspect of the "unrealism" of ideals. When thinking about an ideal, one should never forget these other considerations that stand in the way of its actualization. To return to a previous example, a car's "safety" is a prime desideratum. But it would be foolish to contrive a "perfectly safe" car whose maximum speed is only 1.75 MPH. Safety, speed, efficiency, operating economy, breakdown avoidance, etc. are *all* prime desiderata of a car. Each *counts*, but none *predominates* in the sense that the rest should be sacrificed to it. They must all be combined and coordinated in a good car. The situation with respect to ideals is altogether parallel.

Ideals look to a completion or perfection of some sort. They involve the maximization of sorts, the possession of a mind of some value feature as it is possible to realize. But as the care example shows with many sorts of valued objects involve a plurality of desiderata that constitute a multiparametric value manifold (as per safety, operating economy, reliability, etc. for that autoworker). And in such an authentically multiparametric case there will be no fixed set of exchange: how much of a gain in one value should be seen as balancing off how much of a lapse in another "depends on circumstances"—and in particular on how the other value-parameters stand. The value-contexts at issue here are incommensurable. There is no prospect of any *maximization* here; it is a matter of situation-specific balancing out—of *harmonization* rather than maximization. The idea of ideal completion becomes irrespective here. No ideal outcome is realizable here but only a plurality of alternatives with incommensurable value profiles.

Moreover, ideals do not exist in a vacuum. They do not operate in isolation. They can be pursued only in a complex setting where other "complicating" factors are inevitably also present. For the fact is that even ideals as such compete within one another. Every individual ideal of ours must coexist alongside values within the context provided by an overall "economy" where every element must come to terms with the rest.

Two distinct points must be carefully distinguished. The first is the simple and essentially *economic* point that in a world of limited resources, we must make choices—we cannot have our cake and eat it too. This point of obvious (though not, to be sure, thereby unimportant). The second point, which is a more subtle one, is that the realities of the world are such that the pursuit of ideals is inherently limited by the inevitably *interactive* nature of things. With weight reduction, we increase the operating economy of a car at the sacrifice of its safety. Other things equal, one value factor is generally enhanced at the expense of another. In the political domain, for example, both public order and individual freedom are legitimate values. Yet the interests of the one can in general be advanced only at the cost of the other, lest liberty degenerate into a license to injure the interests of one's fellows. Different aspects of an "imperfect world" are at issue: in the one case, we have to do with man's limited resources, while in the other, we are dealing with man's limited power, with the fact that even were our resources unlimited, there would nevertheless remain drastic, nature-imposed limits to the extent to which man's wish and will can be imposed on the realities of the world.

Ideals look to a completion or perfection. They involve the maximization of sorts, the possession of as much of some value feature as it is possible to realize. But, as the automobile example shows, many sorts of valued objects involve a plurality of desiderata that constitute internally diversified manifold of values (as per safety, operating economy, reliability, etc. for that auto). And in such an authentically multiparametric case there will be no fixed set of exchange: how much of a gain in one value should be seen as balancing off how much of a lapse in another "depends on circumstances"—and in particular on how matters stand with the other value-parameters at issue. The different facets of value that become relevant are incommensurable. Here optimization is a matter of situation-specific balancing out—of *harmonization* rather than maximization. Ideality will now admit of a variety of different realizations.

Ideals can be pursued only within *the limits of the possible* in a complex and no doubt imperfect world. In practice, we have to content ourselves with subideal achievements. It is a key aspect of rationality—of ends-oriented intelligence—that it involves a coming to terms with this fact that considerations of "realism" must temper our dedication to ideals.

Critical obstacles of two different sorts lie in the way of the realization of ideals: the theoretical and the practical.

The theoretical block to realizing idealities roots in the fact that nay ideal involves a plurality of desiderata and that they are always involved in conflicts with one another. And ideal house must be both roomy and convenient via a compactness that conflicts with roominess. An ideal car must be both safe and economical, but safety requires a variety of arrangements and devices all of which cost money. An ideal vacation must afford both change and comfort which stands at odds with one another. And so on. We live in a difficult world where we can only secure more of one elucidation at the expense of forgoing some of another.

The practical blockage to ideal realization lies in the inevitable limitation of our resources. Getting closer to obtaining an ideal—with pretty much any sort of ideal—calls for an increasing expenditure of scarce resources—money, time, effort, what have you. And we live in an uncooperative world where we inevitably have only so much of such resources at our disposal. This means that in the pursuit of any sort of ideal there is only one realistic alternative at out disposal—compromise. We have no choice but to be realistic about it.

V. Ideals and Unrealism

The fact that our ideals and values limit one another in actual operation has important consequences. It means that while ideals can-nay should—be cultivated, they never deserve total dedication and absolute priority, because this would mean an unacceptable sacrifice of other ideals. Their pursuit must be conditioned by recognizing the existence of a point of no advantage, where going further would produce unacceptable sacrifices else-where, and thus prove counterproductive in the larger scheme of things.

In the pursuit of ideals, *unrealism* is thus the constant danger. There is an object lesson to be learned from the case of the man so intent on the cultivation of his pet ideal that he fails to realize that it may cease to be worthwhile when its pursuit blocks the way to other desiderata. Such unrealism is implicit in the pejorative connotation that an "idealistic" person is also naive in having an exaggerated and unrealistic view of the extent to which an ideal can actually be brought to realization without producing untoward "side effects."

Ideals aim at the superlative. When we contemplate the ideal state of something, we envision something we deem to be the very best of possible alternatives in this regard. But given that we can never realize an ideal in full it follows that to apply any such principle in practice, we must know which of several feasible nonideal alternatives is to be preferred: we must not only know what is *the best* but also be in a position to determine which of several putative possibilities comes "closer to the ideal." (How far has the beginner come toward learning how to evaluate bridge hands when he is told that the perfect hand consists of the four aces, the four kings, the four queens, and a jack?) Ideals as such are oriented at a maximum. But for their effective cultivation it is the optimum of a balanced accommodation and harmonization that we must seek.

One must have both the "sensitive judgment" and the "practical know-how" needed to effect an appropriate working compromise among one's ideals. Ideals serve to point the way. But this does not resolve the practical choices that confront us in concrete situations. Having a destination is not much help: we must know about life's twists and turns as well. In and of themselves ideals are insufficient to provide the guidance we actually need.

The intelligent cultivation of an ideal requires us to realize that its pursuit can be overdone. Even as we can make the car so safe that we incur an unacceptable sacrifice of (say) its economy of operation, so we can emphasize individual liberty in the state to such a degree as to compromise public order, etc. Even in cultivating ideals there comes a point of counterproductiveness where "the better is the enemy of the good." An ideal whose pursuit in the prevailing circumstances cannot be carried on in a plausible and sensible way itself thereby becomes inappropriate in those circumstances.

The stress on ideals must accordingly be tempered by this recognition of the need to harmonize and balance values off against one another. In the realm of values, too, there must be a Leibnizian *harmonia rerum* where things are adjusted in an order of mutual compossibility. And a very important difference thus exists between a *compromise* of one's ideals and a *betrayal* of them.

Compromise occurs in the cultivation of an ideal when one tempers or limits its further pursuit because its interaction with other values requires some mutual accommodation—to press further with the supposedly "compromised" ideal in the prevailing circumstances would frustrate our other equally valid objectives. In this regard the compromise of ideals is inevitable, "realistic," and nowise reprehensible. Our "idealistic" dedication to ideals must be tempered by a "realistic" recognition that we must be prepared to settle for less—that our expectations can properly fall short of our aspirations. In all negotiations there is some element of compromise, and the pursuit of ideals proceeds amid a complex negotiation with the difficult circumstances of human life. There is nothing wrong with entering upon such a negotiation with substantial, perhaps inflated, demands. But if we are sensible, we shall do this in the full recognition that in this context, too, we must eventually "settle for less."

CHAPTER TWO

THE MECHANISM OF IDEALIZATION: TRUTH CONDITIONS VERSUS USE CONDITIONS

I. Ideal Surrogacy

The problem with ideals is of course posed by the obvious obstacles we face in a difficult world whose actual realities are inevitably bound to fall short of the ideal.

So how are we to operate with those idealizations in a difficult, complex, imperfect world that does not allow ideals to be brought to actualization as such? How can we ever apply such concepts in a setting that does not put idealities at our disposal? Or do they constitute a useless fifth wheel that spins idly with no work to do?

By no means! For even though outright idealities are unavailable as such, they will—or can—nevertheless be able to accomplish communicative work for us if we allow use conditions to stand surrogate from truth conditions. If an ideal-envisioning concept is to have any sort of use in application we need to operate by means of an achievable approximation to that unrealizable idealization. We need, in sum, to have an achievable surrogate for that unachievable perfection. We must, in sum, not require achieving the ideal but rest content with approximating it as best we can.

And so in actual practice—in the way we actually proceed in communication—what we do—and are understood by our interlocutors as doing—is to conform our linguistic practice to suitable surrogates that indicate an approximation to the relevant ideals. What we have in view is the realization of a certain ideal, but what we use instead is a functional surrogate—a practical placeholder.

And the rationale for this recourse to ideal surrogacy is straightforwardly inherent in the classical principle that necessity knows no bounds (*necessitas non novit lex*). For those ideals are eminently useful communicative resources that facilitate the compact indication of states of affairs—even as we can avoid a complex inventory of his assets and liabilities as a husband by specifying that "he is almost an ideal husband" or "he is the very opposite of an ideal husband." Deployment of idealization concepts spares us endless complexities of qualification and enormously simplifies and facilitates the business of communication.

Nevertheless, in order to put those ideality-purporting concepts to work we need to adopt realistic conditions of application. Given that a difficult and complex reality does not afford justification, we need to approximate, to compromise, to settle for the less than perfect. Just as in dealing with the idea of a flat table top or a straight round we have to contemplate a certain looseness, a depictive for *perfect* straightness and *perfect* flatness, so with these perfection-envisioning concepts must we engage in "compromise."

And so what we actually do in practice is not to insist upon determinate perfectionism as such, but to allow some weaker surrogate to take its place. So instead of the truth-condition contemplating

true ≡ of totally and completely guaranteed veracity

we use the weaker construal:

true ≅ of amply evidentiated veracity

Or again, instead of

desirable ≡ totally nothing to being deemed by fully rational people

we use

desirable ≅ generally desired by sensible people.

And similarly instead of

just ≡ regularly is true with a completely appropriate allocation

we use:

just ≅ generally in line with an appropriate allocation.

It is not that such surrogacy is what the term at issue *means*: that is given by its ambitiously totalitarian specification. It is, rather, that in applying that term we generally make do with that more modest and realistically realizable specification.

It is not that general approbation is what "desirable" *means* or that general endorsement is what "truth" means. It is we in practice allow those less stringent requirements to stands surrogate for the unachievably demanding requirements that are literally at issue with these the idealized terms at issue.

We are not dealing with *definitions* (rigorously accurate specifications of meaning). But rather with *use-conditions*—standards governing the accessible way of applying the terminology context of its commonplace employment.

Let us see how this way of proceeding works out in practice when we effectively allow the resource of use conditions to afford us a means for letting a realizable set of conditions and circumstances serve as a discourse-facilitating surrogate for that which, from other points of view, is simply an unrealizable ideal.

II. Truth and Use Conditions

Ideals and idealizations are purposive instruments. And they function in a particular and particularly important role in linguistic communication because totalities are more graphic than partialities and purities more straightforward than mixtures. Ideals afford guidance even where they look to an unrealizable completeness. To see how this idea plays itself out we must go back to some fundamental features of linguistic communication.

Any adequate theory of language must come to terms with the difference between semantics and pragmatics by acknowledging the crucial distinction between use conditions and truth conditions. The use conditions encompass *the user-oriented circumstances in which a sentence is appropriately and warrantedly assertable by those who employ the particular language* in which it figures. The truth conditions, by contrast, detail *the reality-oriented circumstances that must obtain for the claim that is staked to be correct*. The former provide the *operational criteria* for making the assertion at issue; the latter indicate the entire range of the *objective circumstances* that must obtain for the statement to be made *correctly* (i.e., truly)—always including the whole gamut of inferential consequences that must be taken to follow from its assertion.

The *truth conditions* look to the circumstances that have to obtain for a statement to be correct—as, for example, "There are no witches," coordinates with a world without witches. The truth conditions of a statement accordingly incorporate the sum total of what must be the case for that initial statement to be true. On this basis, any claim whatever that is logically entailed by a given contention will figure among its truth conditions.

By contrast, the *use conditions* of a language comprise the *authorizing criteria for making the assertions at issue* by specifying the sorts of cognitive or epistemic circumstances that qualify a statement as being made by its assertor *appropriately* (i.e., warrantedly). These conditions look to the circumstances under which someone's staking those claims is in order—including what sorts of further circumstances would abrogate such entitlements.[8] They encompass not just the evidential situation but also the general setting of the communicative circumstances in which a particular assertion is validated as appropriate within the setting of the communicative practice at issue. Accordingly, communication policy plays the pivotal role in this context. For while truth conditions deal with the objective facts, use conditions deal with the linguistic properties. If it looks like a duck and quacks like a duck I am within my rights in so calling it.

The use conditions determine the evidential situations in which a statement can appropriately be claimed to obtain—as is certainly the case in the present state of general knowledge about witchcraft and its ways. When I see what looks to be an apple in the grocer's bin next to a label reading "Fresh Macintoshes, 30¢ per pound," I quite appropriately take the *use* conditions for the claim "Those objects are apples" to be fully and amply satisfied. But, of course, *truth* conditions are something else again. Their satisfaction requires (among other things) that those objects have apple cores at their middle rather than sand; that they grew on apple trees rather than being synthesized in an apple-replicator; that they are not strangely deformed pears of some sort, and so on without end. We could never manage to ascertain them all.

And the salient point is that the satisfaction of use conditions provides authorization for making a claim in a way the community of language users understand and accepts as responsible and cogent, while satisfaction of (all) the truth conditions is needed to guarantee that the statement is correct. The satisfaction of use conditions is sufficient for authorizing that statement's claim; the satisfaction of truth conditions is necessary for that statement to be true.

What is at issue with truth conditions is something far above and beyond the vastly more modest requirements of use conditions. If the circumstances are such that a proposition's *truth* conditions are not satisfied, then this proposition is false. But if the circumstances are such that a proposition's *use* conditions are not satisfied, then this proposition is not necessarily false, but merely such that its assertion fails to be warranted. No tenable inference about its truth can be made one way or the other. The failure here is not an error of commission but an error of omission—of not properly equipping one's claim with an appropriate grounding. When the use conditions are satisfied in the context of a speaker's claim we might well wind up saying that the speaker had spoken *falsely* but not that the speaker had spoken *inappropriately*, let alone "in reckless disregard to the truth."

III. The Inductive Aspect

To be sure, it would be very mistaken to think of the conditions of use or assertability as consisting in explicitly formalized rules. For in general, what is at issue is not, strictly speaking, a matter of *rules* at all. The use conventions at issue are not always formulated and codified; doubtless they are not fully codifiable, any more than are the rules for hitting a forehand in tennis. What is at issue is a matter of the characterizing a practice, of how-to-do-it guidelines, of the skills and tricks of the linguistic trade of what is learned largely through observation, imitation, and habituation, rather than through mastery of and adherence to explicitly specifiable rules. (There are, obviously, some things we must be able to do without using rules—following rules, for example, or understanding language, since otherwise we would be in the paradoxical situation of needing rules to govern the use of rules.) Language users can observe the proprieties without mastering them in a codified form.

It lies in the very nature of things that use conditions must inevitably differ substantially from truth conditions where statements of objective matter of fact are at issue. However, in employing language to communicate about the world, we have no choice but to settle in practice for letting the former do duty for the latter. Consider the following course of reasoning:

It looks like a duck.
It quacks like a duck.
It waddles like a duck.

Therefore: It is a duck.

This reasoning is clearly not deductively valid. (Mechanical ducks can do all those things as well.) Nor is it enthymematically valid. For any premises we might add that actually manage to close the deductive gap fully and completely—Whatever looks, quacks, and waddles like a duck will actually *be* a duck, for example—will simply not be true. And nothing that we can add by way of epistemically *available*

truth will close the deductive gap. Such tenability as the argument has
it obtains from a certain *practical policy*, namely, *As long as no coun-
terindications come to light, to treat as a duck anything that (sufficiently) behaves like one.* And this is a *praxis* rather than a factual
claim of some sort. We know full well that it is false to claim, Whatever looks, quacks, and waddles like a duck will actually be a duck.
But in ordinary circumstances (in the absence of visible counterindi-
cations) we feel free to implement the policy at issue with an inferential leap, not because in doing so we cannot possibly go wrong, but
rather because we will generally go right.

The experience-ampliating reliance that we place on use conditions is simply part and parcel of an inductive process built into the
praxis of language-use that serves as our instrumentality for communicating with one another about the world we live in. The validation
of these highly presumption-predicated communicative resources is
ultimately pragmatic rather than logico-semantical in nature. Cognitive utility is the crux here.

Without reliance on use conditions as distinct from truth conditions, linguistic communication becomes impracticable. And without
our commitment to a fundamentally inductive stance, use conditions
the warrant for our objective assertions and their assertoric context
cannot be bridged over in any other way. Use conditions are thus
essential to the communicative enterprise.

IV. Semantics, Pragmatics, and the Issue of Meaning

The truth conditions of a statement are a matter of the *semantics* of a
language; the use conditions are a matter of what has come to be
called its *pragmatics*. These use conditions are intrinsic components
of the language—a part of what children learn about the use of their
native tongue at mother's knee. Truth conditions do not have a mo-
nopoly on "meaning"—this concept is broad enough to encompass
both sorts of conditions. After all, the use conditions and their correlative imputational ground rules are every bit as much an aspect of
the meaning of our words as are the truth conditions. These two aspects of meaning (viz. consequences via truth condition and antece-
dents via warranting or use conditions) stand in a symbiotic inter-
twining. A crucial part of learning what a word *means* is to learn how
it is *used*—i.e., to get a working grasp of the types of conditions and
circumstances under which its use in certain ways is *appropriate*.
And here it is necessary to realize that this involves an inductive
component—and implicit view of "the way in which things work in
the world."[9]

But surely, truth conditions are the crucial thing for meaning. Surely you don't really know what a statement means if you don't know fully and exactly what follows from it. This seems altogether plausible—but only because we theorists are so deeply invested in the logical (rather than practical) sense of meaning. Semantics has dominated over pragmatics in recent language studies, but both are needed. Without access to the truth conditions of a statement we would not know exactly what it claims; without access to its use conditions, we would not know when it is actually in order to stake this claim. Neither aspect is dispensable.

The critical fact is that meaning is a comprehensive concept that embraces both semantical and pragmatic issues. To gain an adequate grasp of a language we must learn *both* what follows from its statements and what authorizes them—what conditions allow us to take them to be in order. Any exclusivistic doctrine along the lines of meaning is use, or meaning is a matter of truth conditions, is one-sided, dogmatic, *and* inappropriate in its claim to exclusiveness.

Use conditions accordingly reflect a practical policy of presumption. The legitimation of the practical policy at work here is ultimately the matter of convenience. As is generally the case with practical policies, the process is at bottom a matter of cost-benefit calculations. Language simply could not develop as an effective instrument of communication (information transmission) if the u-to-t transition were not generally feasible.[10]

This idea of such presumptive "taking" is a crucial aspect of our language-deploying discursive practice. For one thing it is the pivot point for the objectivity of language use—for its intensionality (with an S) in point of application to real-world objects. The actual starting point may be no more than, I take myself to be seeing an apple. But we readily go beyond this idea to, I take it to be an apple that I see, and then move beyond this thought to *claim*: I see an apple. And these transitions—this move from experiential subjectivity to our objective and factual claims—find their warrant in the established principles and practices of language use, that is, in these use rules of language. It is not that the apple is somehow *given* to us in "brute experience." (Wilfrid Sellars's critique of "The Myth of the Given" is perfectly in order.) But beyond that mythological *given* there lies the reality of what is in practice *taken* by us: the (putative) reality of what we accept to be so subject to the established use rules of linguistic policy and praxis. The justification of those use rules certainly does not lie in observational evidentiation on the basis of something given, seeing that we simply cannot deploy any experience-transcending "observation" to reach behind experience to the subexperiential reality behind what we had experienced. Rather, than being evidential in *this* sort of way, the justification of those use rules is pragmatic. It lies, that is to say, in considerations of utility—in the effectiveness with which they enable us to realize the relevant purposes of the context, which in this linguistic case comes to the guidance of our own actions and the concerting of those actions through communication with others.

V. The Impact of Idealization

The unavoidable distinction between use conditions and truth conditions, and the great range of its communicative utility, is made dramatically clearer that present context of idealization. For the truth-conditions at issue here are unrealizable: in their very nature as such, they represent an idealization in looking to conditions and circumstances beyond the range of accomplishable actuality. Thus if truth conditions were all we have and their satisfaction alone could validate our claims, then silence would be our only recourse. It is because the far more modest use conditions envision the realistic circumstance of realizable conditions that we are able to put these concepts to work.

Moreover, it is solely due to the distinction between truth conditions and use conditions that unrealizable idealizations are able to play an effective role in linguistic communication. For use conditions alone are able to underwrite idealized claims on the basis of realistic circumstances. But for the fundamental duality of truth conditions and use conditions idealization could not be the eminently useful resource it is.[11] And without recourse to the ideal our communication about the real would become impracticably cumbersome.

CHAPTER THREE

KNOWLEDGE AND IDEALIZATION

I. Communicative Parallax

The fact that real things have hidden depths—that they are cognitively opaque—has important ramifications that reach to the very heart of the theory of communication.

Any particular thing—the moon, for example—is such that two related but critically different versions of it can be contemplated:

    (1)   the moon, the actual moon as it "really" is

and

    (2)   the moon as somebody (you or I or the Babylonians) conceives of it.

The crucial fact to note in this connection is that it is virtually always the former item—the thing itself—that we INTEND to communicate or think (= self-communicate) about, the thing *as it is,* and not the thing *as somebody conceives of it.* Yet we cannot but recognize the justice of Kant's teaching that the "I think" (I maintain, assert, etc.) is an ever-present implicit accompaniment of every claim or contention that we make. This factor of attributability dogs our every assertion and opens up the unavoidable prospect of "getting it wrong."

Ambitious intentions or pretensions to the contrary notwithstanding, all that one can ever actually manage to bring off in one's purportedly fact-assertive discourse is to deliver information about item (2)—to convey what one thinks or conceives to be so. I can readily distinguish the features of (what I take to be) "the real moon" from those of "the moon as *you* conceive of it," but I cannot distinguish them from those of "the moon as *I* conceive of it." And when *I* maintain "The moon is roughly spherical" all that I have successfully managed to deliver to you by way of actual information is "Rescher maintains that the moon is roughly spherical." And there is nothing that can be done to alter this circumstance—it doesn't matter how loudly I bang on the table. If you bind me by the injunction, "Tell me something about the Eiffel Tower, but please don't put before me your beliefs or convictions regarding it; just give me facts about the thing itself, rather than presenting any parts of your conception of it!", you condemn me to the silence of the Lockean *je ne sais quoi*.

Let us employ the phrase *communicative parallax* to signalize this circumstance that throughout one's discourse about things one always INTENDS to convey information about "the actual thing itself" but only MANAGES to disclose facets of one's *conception* of the thing. With optical parallax, *where* you see something to be depends on *where you stand* in regard to it. With communicative parallax *how* you see something to be depends on *how you stand* in regard to it. This parallax reflects an inevitable slippage between intention and accomplishment in all fact-stating or fact-purporting discourse.

Now it is important to realize that it is *not* the case that two *different things* are at issue where we talk of "parallax." It would be a grave mistake of illicit hypostatization to reify "the X as we see it" into a *thing* distinct from the real X. "Harry as I picture him" may be very unlike, and quite different from, "the real Harry," but it is still the real Harry that is the *intended object* of my conception, however little it may do him justice. The world is not populated by many Harrys—the real one, and min, and yours, etc., each answering to our respective (distinct) conceptions of him. "Harry as I conceive of him" may well not exist *as such* but this does not block my conception from having Harry—the *real* Harry—as its object. The star we take ourselves to see (the star "as we see it") is not a different *entity*—a thing distinct from "the real star." It *is* the real star, but seen as somehow displaced from its true position in the scheme of things. And much the same holds where communicative parallax is at issue. Here "the thing itself" that contrasts with "the thing as we conceive of it" is not a *different* thing: it is the very selfsame thing which our conception *intends* to capture. The *distinction* between our moon, say, and that of the Babylonians represents no *difference* in object. We have to espouse the view that only one thing—the moon itself—is at issue, which is, as it were, "seen differently" by different discussants. To bring it on the stage of discussion is not to multiply entities by invoking the membership of a cognitively inaccessible transcendental realm, but simply to employ a distinguishing contrast to give convenient expression to the crucial fact of the potential inadequacy of our conceptions.

To speak of parallax is misleading in one way. For we know what allowances to make for astronomical parallax. We do not—and in the nature of the thing *cannot*—know what allowances to make for *communicative* parallax. We are never in a position to realize *how* our conception of a thing is inadequate—we can only realize *that* it may well be so.[12]

II. The Intentionality of Interpersonal Communication

There is nothing unfortunate or regrettable about the fact of communicative parallax. Quite the reverse, it serves an important and positive function. For it is crucial to the achievement of intersubjective objectivity in discourse.

After all, the teleology of language is nothing mysterious and occult. Language is primarily a purposive instrument whose cardinal aim is the transmission of information for the sake of implementation in action. Language is designed to afford us resources for information storage and mechanisms for the inter-personal exchange of information needed for the coherent pursuit of individual goals and the coordination of effort in the pursuit of common goals. And only the accomplishment-transcending INTENTION to discuss "the thing itself" makes communication possible. If my discourse were directed at *my* moon-conception, we could never lock communicative horns. Two different objects would be at issue. The prospect of agreement and disagreement would vanish and the prospect of interpersonal communication about a common object would vanish with it. Moreover, any trans-historical comparability of objects would go by the board. The sun and moon of the Babylonian priest-astrologers would be as disjoint from ours as are our respective deities. Communicative parallax would be overcome, but at an awesome price—communicative anarchy. The exact configuration of information that I myself have about a thing at first hand is always something personal and idiosyncratic— based upon the contingencies of what I "happen to have experienced" about it and what I "happen to have gathered" about the experience of others. In making objective assertions about something, it is thus crucial that I intend to discuss "the thing itself" rather than "the thing just precisely as I conceive of it" relative to the body of information I have about it. Only the former is something that somebody else can get hold of; the latter certainly is not. The imputational move beyond the data at hand is indispensably demanded by that step into the domain of the publicly accessible objects in whose absence interpersonal communication about a shared world becomes impossible.

This fundamental intention of objectification, the intention to discuss "the moon itself" (the real moon) regardless of how untenable one's own *ideas* about it may eventually prove to be is a basic precondition of the very possibility of communication. It is crucial to the communicative enterprise to take the egocentrism-avoiding stance of an epistemological Copernicanism that rejects all claims to a privileged status for *our own* conception of things. The workings of communicative parallax root in the fact that we are prepared to "discount any misconceptions" (our own included) about things over a very wide range indeed—that we are committed to the stance that factual disagreements as to the character of things are communicatively irrelevant within enormously broad limits. The incorrectness of conceptions is venial.

We are able to say something about the (real) Sphinx because of our submission to a fundamental communicative convention or "social contract:" to the effect that we *intend* ("mean") to talk about it—the very thing itself as it "really" is—our own private conception of it notwithstanding. We arrive at the standard policy that prevails with respect to all communicative convention or "social contract" to the effect that we *intend* ("mean") to talk about it—the very thing itself as it "really" is—our own private conception of it notwithstanding. We arrive at the standard policy that prevails with respect to all communicative discourse of letting "the language we use," rather than whatever specific informative aims we may actually "have in mind" on particular occasions, be the decisive factor with regard to the things at issue in our discourse. When I speak about the Sphinx— even though I do so on the basis of my own conception of what is involved here—I will nevertheless be taken to be discussing "the *real* Sphinx" in virtue of the basic conventionalized intention at issue with regard to the operation of referring terms.

Communication requires not only common *concepts* but common *topics*—shared items of discussion, a common world of selfsubsistently real "an sich" objects basic to shared experience. The factor of objectivity reflects our basic commitment of a shared world as the common property of communicators. Such a commitment involves more than merely *de facto* intersubjective agreement. For such agreement is a matter of *a posteriori* discovery, while our view of the nature of things puts "the real world" on a necessary and *a priori* basis. This stance roots in the fundamental convention of a shared social insistence on communicating—the commitment to an objective world of real things affording the crucially requisite common focus needed for any genuine communication.

Someone might object:

> How can recourse to "the thing itself" possibly facilitate communication? My interlocutor cannot lay hold of this any more than I

can, seeing that it has features transcending anyone's conception
of it. So how can it serve to establish contact between us.

This objection misses the point. We do indeed "lay hold of" the thing
itself—not by way of information, by inquiry or investigation, but *by
fiat or postulation*. Objective knowledge ultimately roots in that
power of *positing* something (*"etwas schlecht hin zu setzen"*) which,
according to Fichte is a characteristic power of the self, the ego of an
intelligent being. What links my discourse with that of my interlocutor is our common subscription to the *a priori* presumption (a defeasible presumption, to be sure) that we are talking in common about a
shared thing, our own possible misconceptions of it notwithstanding.
Communicative parallax assures us of being in touch with one another from the very outset. And it means that no matter how much we
change our mind about the *nature* of a thing (the moon) or type of
thing (the whale), we are still dealing with exactly the same thing or
sort of thing. It assures reidentification across theories and belief-
systems.

Again someone might object:

> But surely we can get by on the basis of personal conceptions
> alone, without invoking the notion of "a thing itself." My concep-
> tion of a thing is something I can convey to you, given enough
> time. Cannot communication proceed by correlating and match-
> ing personal conceptions, without appeal to the intermediation of
> "the thing itself."

But think here of the concrete practicalities. What is "enough time"?
When is the match "sufficient" to underwrite out right identification?
The cash value of our commitment to the thing itself is that it enables
us to make this identification straight away by imputation, by fiat on
the basis of modest indicators, rather than on the basis of an appeal to
the inductive weight of a body of evidence that is always bound to be
problematic. Communication is something *we set out* to do, not something we ultimately discern, with the wisdom of eventual hindsight, to
have accomplished retrospectively.

Nevertheless, these objections make a useful contribution. They
engender recognition that "the thing itself" operative in this discussion is not a peculiar sort of *thing*—a new ontological category—but
rather a shorthand formula for a certain policy of communicative presumption or imputation, namely that of an *a priori* commitment to the
idea of a commonality of objective focus that is to be allowed to stand
unless and until circumstances arise to render this untenable.

The objectifying imputation at issue here lies at the very basis of
our cognitive stance that we live and operate in a world of real and

objective things. This commitment to the idea of a shared real world is crucial for communication. Its status is *a priori:* its existence is not something we learn of through experience. As Kant clearly saw, objective experience is possible only if the existence of such a real, objective world is *presupposed* at the onset rather than seen as a matter of *ex post facto* discovery about the nature of things.

What is at issue here is thus not a matter of *discovery*, but one of *imputation*. The element of community, of identity of focus is not a matter of *ex post facto* learning from experience, but of an *a priori* predetermination inherent in our approach to language-use. We do not *infer* things as being real and objective from our phenomenal data, but establish our perception as authentic perception OF genuine objects through the fact that these objects are given—or rather, *taken*—as real and objectively existing things from the first.[13] Objectivity is not deduced but imputed.

A closer look at the precise character of the justification of our evidence-transcending imputations is in order. The authorizing warrant for the imputational thrust of our objective categorical judgment ultimately resides in the purposive teleology of language-use—the desire for successful communication. It was suggested above that this is simply a matter of this-or-nothing—that if we wish to achieve answers to our questions about the world and if we wish to communicate with one another about matters of objective fact, then we simply have no alternative but to undertake such evidence-transcending commitments. But we now see that this focus on this-or-nothing considerations is by no means the whole story. For the consideration that we *must* proceed in this way—the fact of *practical necessity* that there just is no alternative if our objective is to be reached—stops well short of achieving full adequacy in its justificatory force. It does not offer us any assurance that we actually will succeed in our endeavor if we do proceed in this way; it just has it that we won't if we don't. The issue of actual effectiveness remains untouched. And here we have no choice but to proceed experientially—by the simple stratagem of "trying and seeing." Practical necessity remains a matter of *a priori* considerations, but efficacy—actual sufficiency—will be a matter of *a posteriori* experience. The justification of claims of efficacy emerges through pragmatic retrojustification—a retrospective revalidation in the light of experience. The pragmatic consideration that our praxis of inquiry and communication does actually work—that we can effectively and (by and large) successfully communicate with one another about a shared world, inquiry into whose nature and workings proceeds successfully as a communal project of investigation—is the ultimately crucial consideration that legitimates the evidence-transcending imputations built into the praxis-governing use-conditions of language.

In answering the question of what justifies our recourse to the evidence-transcending imputations we thus proceed at two levels. On the negative side we confront the realization then we *must* accept them; it is this or nothing, given the goals of the enterprise. On the positive side, we involve a pragmatic retrojustification based on the fact that our proceeding in this way underwrites an actually effective praxis.[14]

III. Objectivity as a Requisite of Communication and Inquiry

Objectivity in its particular aspect of cognitive independence, of publicity and autonomy of cognitive status, is essential to our capacity to communicate about things. The information that we may have about a thing, be it real or presumptive information, is always just that—information *we* lay claim to. We recognize that it varies from person to person. Our attempts at communication and inquiry are thus undergirded by an information-transcending stance—the stance that we communally inhabit a shared world of objectively existing things, a world of "real things" amongst which we live and into which we inquire (but about which we do and must presume ourselves to have only imperfect information at any and every particular stage of the cognitive venture). This is clearly not something that we learn from the course of experience. The "facts of experience" can never reveal it to us. It is something we postulate or presuppose. Its epistemic status is not that of an empirical discovery, but that of a presupposition whose ultimate justification is a transcendental argument from the very possibility of the projects of communication and inquiry as we standardly conduct them.

Our commitment to an objective reality that lies behind the data at hand is indispensably demanded by any step into the domain of the publicly accessible objects essential to communal inquiry and interpersonal communication about a shared world. We could not establish communicative contact about a common objective item of discussion if our discourse were geared to the substance of our own idiosyncratic ideas and conceptions. But the objectivity at issue in our communicative discourse is a matter of its *status* rather than one of its *content*. For the substantive content of a claim about the world in no way tells us whether it is factual or fictional. This is something we have to determine from its *context*: it is a matter of the frame, not of the canvas. The fact-oriented basis of our information-transmitting exchanges is provided *a priori* by a conventionalized intention to talk about "the real world." This intention to take real objects to be at issue, objects as they really are, our potentially idiosyncratic conceptions of them quite aside, is fundamental because it is overriding—that is, it overrides all of our other intentions when we enter upon the communicative venture. Without this conventionalized intention we should not be able to convey information—or misinformation—to one another about a shared "objective" world.

We are able to say something about the (real) moon or the (real) Sphinx because of our submission to a fundamental communicative convention or "social contract" to the effect that we *intend* ("mean") to talk about it—that very thing itself as it "really" is—our own private conception of it notwithstanding. We arrive at the standard policy that prevails with respect to all communicative discourse of letting "the language we use," rather than whatever specific informative aims we may actually "have in mind" on particular occasions, be the decisive factor with regard to the things at issue in our discourse. When I speak about the Sphinx (even though I do so on the basis of my own conceivably strange conception of what is involved here), I will be discussing "the *real* Sphinx" in virtue of the basic conventionalized intention governing our use of referring terms.

This fundamental intention of objectification, the intention to discuss "the moon itself" regardless of how untenable one's own *ideas* about it may eventually prove to be is a basic precondition of the very possibility of communication. It is crucial to the communicative enterprise to take the egocentrism-avoiding stance that rejects all claims to a privileged status for *our own* conception of things. In the interests of this stance we are prepared to "discount any misconceptions" (our own included) about things over a very wide range indeed—that we are committed to the stance that factual disagreements as to the character of things are communicatively irrelevant within very broad limits. The incorrectness of conceptions is venial.

If we were to set up our own conception of things as somehow definitive and decisive, we would at once erect a barrier not only to further inquiry but—no less importantly—to the prospect of successful communication with one another. Communication could then only proceed with the wisdom of hindsight—at the end of a long process of tentative checks. Communicative contact would be realized only in the implausible case where extensive exchange indicated retrospectively that there had been an *identity* of conceptions all along. And we would always stand on very shaky ground. For no matter how far we push our investigation into the issue of an identity of conceptions, the prospect of a divergence lying just around the corner—waiting to be discovered if only we pursued the matter just a bit further—can never be precluded. One could never advance the issue of the identity of focus past the status of a more or less well-grounded *assumption*. And then any so-called communication would no longer be an exchange of information but a tissue of frail conjectures. The communicative enterprise would become a vast inductive project—a complex exercise in theory-building, leading tentatively and provisionally toward something which, in fact, the imputational groundwork of our language enables us to presuppose from the very outset.[15]

Communication requires not only common *concepts* but common *topics*, inter-personally shared items of discussion, a common world constituted by the self-subsistently real objects basic to shared experience. The factor of objectivity reflects our basic commitment to a communally available world as the common property of communicators. Such a commitment involves more than merely *de facto* inter-subjective agreement. For such agreement is a matter of *a posteriori* discovery, while our view of the nature of things puts "the real world" on a necessary and *a priori* basis. This stance roots in the fundamental convention of a shared social insistence on communicating—the commitment to an objective world of real things affords the crucially requisite common focus needed for any genuine communication. What links my discourse with that of my interlocutor is our common subscription to the *a priori* presumption (a defeasible presumption, to be sure) that we are both talking about a shared thing, our own possible misconceptions of it notwithstanding. This means that no matter how extensively we may change our minds about the *nature* of a thing or type of thing, we are still dealing with exactly the same thing or sort of thing as before. It assures reidentification across theories and belief-systems.

Our concept of a *real thing* is such that it provides a fixed point, a stable center around which communication revolves, an invariant focus of potentially diverse conceptions. What is to be determinative, decisive, definitive, etc., of the things at issue in my discourse is not my conception, or yours, or indeed anyone's conception at all. The conventionalized intention discussed means that a coordination of conceptions is not decisive for the possibility of communication. Your statements about a thing will convey something to me even if my conception of it is altogether different from yours. To communicate we need not take ourselves to share views of the word, but only take the stance that we share the world being discussed.

The commitment to *objectivity* is basic to any prospect of our discourse with one another about a shared world of "real things," to which none of us is in a position to claim privileged access. This commitment establishes a need to "distance" ourselves from things, that is, to recognize the prospect of a discrepancy between our (potentially idiosyncratic) conceptions of things and the true character of these things as they exist objectively in "the real world." The ever-present contrast between "the thing as we view it" and "the thing as it is" is the mechanism by which this crucially important distancing is accomplished. And maintaining this stance means that we are never entitled to claim to have exhausted a thing *au fond* in cognitive re-gards, to have managed to bring it wholly within our epistemic grasp. For to make this claim would, in effect, be to *identify* "the thing at issue" purely in terms of "our own conception of it," an identification which would effectively remove the former item (the thing itself) from the stage of consideration as an independent entity in its own right, by endowing our conception with decisively determinative force. And this would lead straightaway to the unacceptable result of a cognitive solipsism that would preclude reference to inter-subjectively identifiably particulars, and would thus block the possi-bility of inter-personal communication and communal inquiry.

In communication regarding things we must be able to exchange information about them with our contemporaries and to transmit in-formation about them to our successors. And we must be in a position to do this on the presumption that *their* conceptions of things are not only radically different from *ours*, but conceivably also rightly differ-ent. Thus, it is a crucial precondition of the possibility of successful communication about things that we must avoid laying any claim either to the completeness or even to the ultimate correctness of our own conceptions of any of the things at issue. This renders it critically important *that* (and understandable why) conceptions are not pivotal for communicative purposes. Our discourse *reflects* conceptions and perhaps *conveys* them, but it is not substantively *about* them.

What is crucial for communication, however, is the fundamental intention to deal with the objective order of this "real world." If our assertoric commitments did not transcend the information we have on hand, we would never be able to "get in touch" with others about a shared objective world. No claim is made for the *primacy* of our con-ceptions, or for the *correctness* of our conceptions, or even for the mere *agreement* of our conceptions with those of others. The funda-mental intention to discuss "the thing itself" predominates and over-rides any mere dealing with the thing as we conceive it to be. Cer-tainly, that reference to "objectively real things" at work in our discourse does not contemplate a peculiar sort of *thing*—a new *onto-logical* category of "things-in-themselves." It is simply a shorthand formula for a certain communicative presumption or imputation rooted in an *a priori* commitment to the idea of a commonality of objective focus that is allowed to stand unless and until circumstances arise to render this untenable.

The objectivity at issue in our communicative discourse is a matter of its *status* rather than of its *content*. It is not (necessarily) the substantive content of the work that tells us whether it is factual or fictional, but something we determine from the context (e.g., the introduction or even the dust jacket) before we take up the work itself. It is a matter of the frame, not of the canvas. The fact-oriented basis of our exchanges is a matter of a conventionalized intention, fixed *a priori*, to talk about "the real world."

This intention to take real objects to be at issue, objects as they are in themselves, our potentially idiosyncratic conceptions of them quite aside, is fundamental because it is overriding—that is, it overrides all of our other intentions when we enter upon the communicative venture. Without this conventionalized intention we should not be able to convey information—or misinformation—to one another about a shared "objective" world. We could never establish communicative contact about a common objective item of discussion if our discourse were geared to the things as conceived of in terms of our own specific information about them.

This ever-operative contrast between "the thing itself" and "the thing as we ourselves take it to be" means that we are never in a position to claim definitive finality for our conception of a thing. We are never entitled to claim to have exhausted it *au fond* in cognitive regards—that we have managed to bring it wholly within our epistemic grasp. For to make this claim would, in effect, be to *identify* "the thing itself" in terms of "our own conception of it," an identification which would effectively remove the former item (the thing itself) from the stage of consideration as an independent entity in its own right by endowing our conception with decisively determinative force. And this would lead straightaway to the unpleasant result of a cognitive solipsism that would preclude reference to intersubjectively identifiable particulars, and would thus block the possibility of interpersonal communication.

The commitment of *objectivity* is basic to our discourse with one another about a shared world of "real things" to which none of us is in a position to claim privileged access. This commitment establishes a need to "distance" ourselves from things—i.e., to recognize the prospect of a discrepancy between our (potentially idiosyncratic) conceptions of things and the true character of these things as they exist objectively in "the real world." The ever-present contrast between "the thing as we view it" and "the thing as it is" is the mechanism by which this crucially important distancing is accomplished.

IV. The Communicative Irrelevance of Conceptions

Any pretensions to the predominance, let alone the correctness of our own conceptions regarding the furniture of this realm must be put aside in the context of communication. The fundamental intention to deal with the objective order of this "real world" is crucial. If our assertoric commitments did not transcend the information we ourselves have on hand, we would never be able to "get in touch" with others about a shared objective world. No claim is made for the *primacy* of our conceptions, or for the *correctness* of our conceptions, or even for the mere *agreement* of our conceptions with those of others. The fundamental intention to discuss "the thing itself" predominates and overrides any mere dealing with the thing as we ourselves conceive of it.

If we were to set up our own conception as somehow definitive and decisive, we would at once erect a grave impediment to the prospect of successful communication with one another. Communication could then only proceed retrospectively with the wisdom of the hindsight. It would be realized only in the implausible case that extensive exchange indicates that there has been an *identity* of conceptions all along. We would then learn only by experience—at the end of a long process of wholly tentative and provisional exchange. And we would always stand on very shaky ground. For no matter how far we push our inquiry into the issue of an identity of conceptions, the prospect of a divergence lying just around the corner—waiting to be discovered if only we pursued the matter just a bit further—can never be precluded. One could never advance the issue of identity of focus past the status of a more or less well-grounded *assumption*. And then any so-called communication is no longer an exchange of information but a tissue of frail conjectures. The communicative enterprise would become a vast inductive project—a complex exercise in theory-building, leading tentatively and provisionally toward something which, in fact, the imputational groundwork of our language enables us to presuppose from the very outset.[16]

The fact that we need not agree on our conceptions of things means, *a fortiori*, that we need not be correct in our conceptions of things to communicate successfully about them. This points, in part, to the trivial fact that I need not agree with what you are saying to understand you. But it points also, more importantly, to the consideration that my having a conception of a thing massively different from yours will not prevent me from taking you to be talking about the same thing that I have in mind. Objectivity and referential commonality of focus are matters of initial presumption or presupposition. The issue here is not with what *is* understood, but with what *is to be* understood (by anybody) in terms of a certain generalized and communicative intentions. (The issue here is not one of *meaning* but only of *meaningfulness*.)

Our concept of a *real thing* is accordingly such that a thing is a fixed point, a stable center around which communication revolves, the invariant focus of potentially diverse conceptions. What is to be determinative, decisive, definitive, (etc.) of the things at issue in my discourse is not my conception, or yours, or indeed anyone's conception at all. The conventionalized intention discussed above means that: a coordination of conceptions is not decisive for the possibility of communication. Your statements about a thing will convey something to me even if my conception of it is altogether different from yours. To communicate we need not "think alike"—we need not take ourselves to share views of the word, but only to take the stance that we share the world being discussed.

In communication regarding things we must be able to exchange information about them with our contemporaries and to transmit information about them to our successors. And we must be in a position to do this in the face of the presumption that *their* conceptions of things are not only radically different from *ours*, but conceivably also rightly different. What is at issue here is not the commonplace that we do not know *everything* about anything. Rather, the key consideration is the more interesting thesis that it is a crucial precondition of the possibility of successful communication about things that we must avoid laying any claim either *to the completeness or even to the ultimate correctness of our own conceptions* of any of the things at issue.

It is crucial that the mechanisms of human communication should lie within the domain of human power—they could not otherwise be what they are. Now with respect to the *meanings of words* this condition is satisfied, because this is something that we ourselves fix by custom or by fiat. But *the correctness of conceptions* is not simply a matter of human discretion—it is something that lies outside the sphere of our effective control. For a "correct conception" is akin to Spinoza's *true idea* of which he stipulates that it must "agree with its object"[17]—in circumstances where this issue of agreement may well elude us. (Man proposes but does not dispose with respect to this matter of idea/actuality coordination.) We do, no doubt, *purport* our conceptions to be correct, but whether this is indeed so is something we cannot tell with assurance until "all the returns are in"—that is, never. This fact renders it critically important *that* (and understandable *why*) conceptions are communicatively irrelevant. Our discourse *reflects* our conceptions and perhaps *conveys* them, but it is not substantive *about* them.

The conception of a thing may be the vehicle of thought, but it is never the determinant of reference. By their very nature, conceptions are too personal—and thus potentially too idiosyncratic—for our communicative needs. For communication, interpersonal and public instrumentalities are indispensably requisite. And language affords this desideratum. It provides the apparatus by which the *identity* of the referents of our discourse becomes fixed, however imperfectly we ourselves perceive their nature. (The specifications of things as enshrined in language are Kripkean "rigid designators" in an *epistemic* manner: our indicators for real-things-in-the-world are *designed* in both senses, constructed and intended to perform—insofar as possible—an invariant identificatory job across the diversified spectrum of epistemic worlds.)

How do we really know that Anaximander was talking about *our* sun? He is not here to tell us. He did not leave elaborate discussion about his aims and purposes. How can we be so confident of what he meant to talk about? The answer is straightforward. That he is *to be taken* to talk about *our* sun is, in something that turns, the final analysis, on two very general issues in which Anaximander himself plays little if any role at all: (1) our subscription to certain generalized principles of interpretation with respect to the Greek language, and (2) the conventionalized subscription by us and ascription to other language-users in general of certain fundamental communicative policies and intentions. In the face of appropriate functional equivalences we allow neither a difference in language nor a difference or "thought-worlds" to block an identity of reference.[18]

The pivotal INTENTION to communicate about a common object—resigning any and all claims to regard our own conceptions of it as definitive (decisive)—is the indispensable foundation of all communication. And this intention is not something personal and idiosyncratic—a biographical aspect of certain particular minds—it is a shared feature of "social mind," built into the use of language as a publicly available communicative resource. The wider social perspective is crucial. In subscribing to the conventionalized intention at issue, we sink "our own point of view" in the interests of entering into the wider community of fellow communicators. Only be admitting the potential distortion of one's own conceptions of things through "communicative parallax" can one manage to reach across the gulf of divergent conceptions so as to get into communicative touch with one another.

The information that we may have about a thing—be it real or presumptive information—is always just that, viz. information that WE lay claim to. We cannot but recognize that it is person-relative and in general person-differentiated. Our attempts at communication and inquiry are thus undergirded by an information-transcending stance—the stance that we communally inhabit a shared world of objectively existing things—a world of "real things" amongst which we live and into which we inquire but about which we do and must presume ourselves to have only imperfect information at any and every particular stage of the cognitive venture. This is not something we learn. The "facts of experience" can never reveal it to us. It is something we postulate or presuppose. Its epistemic status is not that of an empirical discovery, but that of a presupposition that is a product of a transcendental argument for the very possibility of communication or inquiry as we standardly conceive of them.

We thus arrive at the key idea which these lines of thought contribute to the present deliberations. True enough, cognitive change carries conceptual change in its wake. But nevertheless—and this point is crucial—we have an ongoing commitment to a manifold of objective *things* that are themselves impervious to conceptual and cognitive change. This commitment is built into the very ground-rules that govern our use of language and embody our determination to maintain the picture of a relatively stable world amidst the ever-changing panorama of cognitive world-pictures. The continuing succession of the different states of science are all linked to a pre-or sub-scientific view of an ongoing "real world" in which we live and work, a world portrayed rather more stably in the *lingua franca* of everyday-life communication and populated by shared things whose stability amidst cognitive change is something rather *postulated* than learned. This postulation reflects the realistic stance that the things we encounter in experience are the *subject* and not the *product* of our inquiry.

V. Scientific Versus Ordinary-Life Communication

It is useful to bear in mind that different priorities obtain in different contexts of communication. In everyday-life communication where we are deeply concerned to protect our credibility, we value security over informativeness. Hence looseness and imprecision are perfectly acceptable. On the other hand, in science, we value generality and precision over security. After all, natural science is not content with these like, *On the whole, larger objects are heavier, or most things made predominantly of lead generally melt at temperatures around 330 degrees Celsius.* In science, we seek exactness and precision: we want to know how all objects of exactly this or that sort always behave. Generality, precision, detail are at a premium, and so in scientific discourse we prioritize these factors in a way that makes our sci-

entific theories vulnerable. (The half-life of theories in frontier physics is relatively short.)

It is of the nature of natural science at the research frontier that it
aims to characterize nature's processes exactly and to describe how
they operate always and everywhere, in full generality and precise
detail. Technical science forswears the looseness of vague generality
or analogy or approximation. It has no use for qualifiers such as usually, normally, or typically; universality and exactness are its touch-
stones. Science, accordingly, declares not merely that roughly such-
and-such generally occurs in certain sorts of circumstances, but exactly what happens in exactly what circumstances. In science we always aim at the maximum of universality, precision, and exactness.
The law claims of science involve no hedging, no fuzziness, no incompleteness, and no exceptions; they are strict: precise, wholly explicit, exceptionless, and unshaded. In making the scientific assertion,
"The melting point of lead is 327.7 degrees Celsius," we mean to
assert that *all* pieces of (pure) lead will unfailingly melt at *exactly* this
temperature. We certainly do not mean to assert that most pieces of
(pure) lead will *probably* melt at *somewhere around* this temperature.
(And in this regard, there would be a potential problem, should it turn
out, for example, that there is no melting point at all and that what is
actually at issue is the center of a statistical distribution.) And this
commitment to generality and detailed precision renders the claims of
science highly vulnerable. We realize that none of the hard claims of
present-day frontier natural science will move down the corridors of
time untouched. Fragility is the price that we pay in science for the
sake of generality and precision.

Increased confidence in the correctness of our estimates can always be purchased at the price of decreased accuracy. We *estimate*
the height of the tree at around 25 feet. We are *quite sure* that the tree
is 25±5 feet. We are *virtually certain* that its height is 25±10 feet. But
we are *completely and absolutely sure* that its height is between 1
inch and 100 yards. Of this we are completely sure, in the sense that
we deem it absolutely certain, certain beyond the shadow of a doubt,
as certain as we can be of anything in the world, so sure that we
would be willing to stake our life on it, and the like. With any sort of
estimate, there is always a characteristic trade-off relationship between the evidential *security* of the estimate on the one hand (as determinable on the basis of its probability or degree of acceptability),
and its contentual *definiteness* (exactness, detail, precision, etc.) on
the other.

This relationship between security and definiteness is generally
characterized by a curve of the general form of an equilateral hyper-
bola: $s \times d = c$ (c = constant). (See Display 2.) The increased vulner-

ability and diminished security of our claims is the inescapable other side of the coin of the pursuit of definiteness. Science operates in the lower right-hand sector of the figure. Its cultivation of informativeness (definiteness of information) entails the risk of error in science: its claims are subject to great insecurity. No doubt the progress of science makes it possible to decrease the value of c somewhat, but the fundamental trade-off relationship remains unavoidable. An information-theoretic uncertainty principle prevents our obtaining the sort of information we would ideally like.[19] The exactness of technical scientific claims makes them especially vulnerable, notwithstanding our most elaborate efforts at their testing and substantiation.

Display 2

THE RELATIONSHIP BETWEEN SECURITY AND
DEFINITENESS

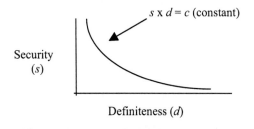

Definiteness (d)

The situation in science accordingly differs markedly from that which prevails in everyday life. When we ordinarily assert that peaches are delicious, we are asserting something like, Most people will find the eating of suitably grown and duly matured peaches a rather pleasurable experience. Such a statement has all sorts of built-in safeguards, such as *more or less, in ordinary circumstance, by and large, normally, if all things are equal,* and so on. They are nothing like scientific laws but mere rules of thumb, a matter of practical lore rather than scientific rigor. And this enables them to achieve great security, for there is safety in vagueness: a factual claim can always acquire security through inexactness. Take the claims, There are rocks in the world and Dogs can bark. It is virtually absurd to characterize such everyday-life generalizations as fallible. Their security lies in their indefiniteness or looseness; it is unrealistic and perverse to characterize such common-life claims as defeasible. They say so little that it is unthinkable that contentions such as these should be overthrown. And this accords smoothly with the needs of the situation. For ordinary-life communication is a practically oriented endeavor carried on in a social context. It stresses such maxims as: Aim for security, even at the price of definiteness; Protect your credibility; Avoid misleading people.

When, as in ordinary life, the preservation of credibility is paramount, one wants to formulate one's claims in as safe and secure a way as possible, and thus one resorts to vagueness and imprecision. On the other hand when, as in science, creativity and originality are paramount, then one would put one's claims in the most ambitious and surprising way, accepting the risks inherent in universality, precision, and the like. Plausibly enough, the appropriateness of an epistemic policy hinges upon the nature of the governing desideratum (credibility vs. creativity).

The aims of ordinary-life discourse are primarily practical, largely geared to social interaction and the coordination of human effort in communal enterprises that serve the common good. In this context, it is crucial that we aim at credibility and acceptance—that we establish and maintain a good reputation for reliability and trustworthiness. In the framework of common-life discourse, we thus take our stance at a point far removed from that of science. Very different probative orientations prevail in the two areas. In everyday contexts, our approach is one of situational satisfying: we stop at the first level of sophistication and complexity that suffices for our present needs. In science, however, our objectives are primarily theoretical and governed by the aims of disinterested inquiry. Hence the claims of informativeness—of generality, exactness, and precision—are paramount.

In science, we accept greater risks willingly because we ask much more of the project. We deliberately court risk by aiming at maximal definiteness and thus at maximal informativeness and testability. Aristotle's view that terrestrial science deals with what happens ordinarily and in the normal course of things has long ago been left by the wayside. The theories of modern natural science has little interest in what happens generally or by and large; they seek to transact their explanatory business in terms of strict universality, in terms of what happens always and everywhere and in all kinds of circumstances. And in consequence we have no choice but to acknowledge the vulnerability of our scientific statements, subject to the operation of the security-definiteness trade-off.

In ordinary life, we operate at the upper left-hand side of the Display 2 curve. The situation contrasts sharply with that of science, whose objectives are largely theoretical, and where the name of the game is rigorous understanding on a basis of unrestricted universality and extreme precision. The cost-benefit situation of the two domains is drastically different. Either way, however, an important fact remains constant. Communication about commonly accessible objects rests on certain assumptions and conventions and postulations. (For example: "There is a reality out there which in fact has certain characteristics about which others are trying to tell as something.") The use of such postulations becomes justified retrospectively in due course—yet not be establishing their truth but rather through considerations of utility—of efficiency and economy in the context of a pursuit of our own epistemic purposes.

But in science, the situation is different. Here the process of idealization takes a much firmer hold. Since our cognitive endeavors aspire at one and the same time *both* to security *and* to definiteness, they look to an unrealizable state of things in a away that calls for an inevitable element of idealization.

CHAPTER FOUR

SCIENTIFIC TRUTH AS AN IDEALIZATION

I. Ideal Coherence

The realization of truth at the level of precision and generality that is at issue in science is itself an idealization. For the objectives at issue in scientific theorizing do not in fact admit of a full realization. And the coherentist approach that lies at the basis of an "inductive" reasoning in scientific-matters is unavoidably predicted seeing the relation between our estimative truth-criteriology and the actual truth of the matter as one that must be seen in terms of idealization.

In general terms, a coherence epistemology of truth is one that proceeds on the basis of the truth criterion to the effect that a proposition p is true iff it forms part of an appropriately formed set of optimally coherent propositions. On such an approach, the truth-status that is accorded to propositions reflects not a strictly local aspect of their own, but an ultimately global feature of their place in a larger context: it is not an isolated but a contextual characteristic.

A common objection to the coherence theory of factual truth is that the linkage of coherence to truth is simply too loose for coherence to provide the definitive standard of truth. As one writer put it some years ago:

> It is quite conceivable that the coherence theory is a description of how the truth or falsehood of statements comes to be known rather than an analysis of the meaning of "true."[20]

Here we have the standard reservation regarding a coherence theory of truth: "Coherence may perhaps be suitable as a *criterion* for the true, but certainly not as a *definitional standard* of truth."[21]

It can, however, be shown that if one is prepared to consider coherence in an *idealized* perspective—as *optimal* coherence with a *perfected* data base, rather than as a matter of *manifest* coherence with the *actual* data at our disposal—then an essential link between truth and coherence emerges.

Supporters of a coherentist standard of truth must be able to establish that this criterion is duly consonant with the definitional nature of
truth. For there ought rightfully to be a *continuity* of operation between our evidential criterion of acceptability-as-true and the "truth"
as definitionally specified. Any really satisfactory criterion must be
such as to yield the real thing—at any rate in sufficiently favorable
circumstances. Fortunately for coherentism, it is possible to demonstrate rigorously that truth is tantamount to ideal coherence—that a
proposition's being true is in fact *equivalent* to its being optimally
coherent with an ideal data base.[22]

This circumstance has far-reaching implications. Given that "the
real truth" is guaranteed only by ideal coherence, we have no categorical assurance of the actual correctness of our coherence-guided
inquiries, which are, after all, always incomplete and imperfect. This
is amply substantiated by the history of science, which already shows
that the "discoveries" about how things work in the world secured
through scientific coherentism constantly require adjustment, correction, replacement. It is only too obvious that we cannot say that our
coherence-grounded scientific theorizing furnishes us with the real
(definitive) truth, but just that it furnishes us with the best estimate of
the truth that we can achieve in the circumstances at hand.

In characterizing a claim as true, we indicate that what it states
corresponds to the facts, so that its assertion is in order. But while this
factually ("stating which is the case," "corresponding to the facts") is
what truth is all about, we cannot apply or implement it as such: it
does not provide a basis on which the truth of claims can be determined. Thus while we have the equation

> to be true = to be (assertible as) factually correct

we also will have

> to be determinable as true = capacity to meet certain conditions
> that can be taken as indicators of factual correctness.

But these conditions of truth-determination are in their very nature
conditions whose full realization is a matter of idealization—that is,
the conditions are such as to obtain only in ideal circumstances.

As noted above, it is of the traditional objections to coherentism
in that the coherence theory is unable to deal with the "problem of
error"—to be able to explain how it is that what is *thought* to be true
might yet actually prove false. But, of course, the consideration that
truth is a matter of *ideal* (rather than actually realized) coherence at
once sweeps this difficulty aside.

Definitive knowledge—as opposed to "merely putative" knowledge—is the fruit of *perfected* inquiry. Only here, at the idealized level of perfected science, could we count on securing the real truth about the world that "corresponds to reality" as the traditional phrase has it. Factual knowledge at the level of generality and precision at issue in scientific theorizing is akin to a *perfect* circle. Try as we will, we cannot quite succeed in producing it. We do our best and call the result knowledge—even as we call that carefully drawn "circle" on the blackboard a *circle*. But we realize full well that what we currently call scientific knowledge is no more authentic (perfected) knowledge than what we call a circle in a geometry diagram is an authentic (perfected) circle. Our "knowledge" is in such cases no more than our *best estimate* of the truth of things. Lacking the advantage of a God's-eye view, we have no access to the world's facts save through the mediation of (inevitably incomplete and thus always potentially flawed) *inquiry*. All we can do—and what must suffice us because indeed it is *all* that we can do—is to do the best we can with the cognitive state of the art to *estimate* "the correct" answers to our scientific questions.

I. The "Continuity Condition" Relating a Criterion to the Definition of Truth

The real and authentic truth as such is something absolute that admits no admixture of qualification or correction. In matters of real-world inquiry it is, thus an idealization. But in actual practice in our communicative affairs, coherence with environing information stands useconditionally surrogate for it. But how can this sort of compromise be justified?

The standard objection to the coherence theory of factual truth is that the linkage of informative coherence to actual factuality is simply too loose for coherence to provide the definitive standard of truth: "Coherence may perhaps be suitable as a criterion for the true, but certainly not as a definitional standard of truth." As one philosopher has put it:

> One might agree that a given statement is accepted as true in virtue of standing in certain logical relations to other statements; still it would not follow that in calling it true one *means* to ascribe to it those relations.[23]

The aim of the present deliberations it to show that this line of objection is untenable.

Our theme, then, is the controverted issue of whether the bearing of coherence is limited to its potential role as a mere *criterion of factual truth*, or whether coherence somehow inheres in the definition of truth by reflecting an *essential aspect of its nature*.[24] However, if one is prepared to consider coherence in an *idealized* perspective—as *optimal* coherence with a *perfected* data base, rather than as a matter of apparent coherence with the imperfect data we actually have in hand—then an essential link between truth and coherence emerges.[25]

Supporters of a coherentist standard of truth must be able to establish that this criterion is duly consonant with the definitional nature of truth. For there ought rightfully to be a *continuity* of operation between our evidential criterion of acceptability-as-true and the "truth" as definitionally specified. Any really satisfactory criterion must be such as to yield the real thing—at any rate in sufficiently favorable circumstances. Fortunately for coherentism, it is possible to demonstrate rigorously that truth is tantamount to ideal coherence—that a proposition's being true is in fact *equivalent* to its being optimally coherent with an ideal data-base.

This requirement that true theses are coextensive with beliefs that are criteriologically justified in ideal circumstances might be characterized as "the continuity condition." A bit of symbolism will be helpful in providing its precise formulation:

$C(S/f)$ is to stand for: the statement S satisfies the truth-criterion C given that circumstances f obtain;

$I(S)$ is to stand for: (epistemically) ideal circumstances with respect to the statement S.

Given these specifications, the continuity condition now reads as follows:

If C is to constitute an adequate criterion of truth, then it must be demonstrably the case that for any statement S, the truth of S is tantamount to its satisfying C under ideal evidential conditions with respect to S. We thus have: is true iff $C(S/I(S))$.

It is the demand for this sort of idealization relationship which is at issue in Brand Blanshard's right-minded insistence that "a 'logical gap' so broad that a criterion and what it is supposed to indicate may each be present in the absence of the other surely falls short of the trustworthiness required of a criterion."[26]

Accordingly, to validate a coherent criteriology we must be able to show that, at least ideally, if we abstract from the imperfections of messy real-life situations, coherence does indeed get at "the real truth of things." This, then is the thesis we have to demonstrate.

A preliminary point needs to be made. If C is to serve as our operative criterion of truth, then we shall have it that C-satisfaction in the prevailing epistemic circumstances suffices—in the manner of use-conditions—to underwrite acceptance as true. In effect we thus have:

> If $C(S/A)$, where A represents the actually prevailing circumstances, then S is true.

Commitment to this implication follows at once from our adoption of C as a criterion of truth. But this condition, of course, only reflects a practical policy of ours, inherent in subscribing to C as a criterion of truth: it merely expresses our determination to accept S as true when C is actually satisfied. What is at issue here is not an abstract general principle, but only our adherence to a certain *modus operandi*. And there is, of course, the prospect of a slip between cup and lip here, since the actual circumstances, A, may be far from ideal for S. that "practical policy" at issue comes down to the rough and ready posture that the prevailing circumstances are good enough—that the "data on hand" are sufficient to permit us to decide the matter. On the other hand, the continuity criterion—S is true if and only if $C(S/I(S))$—represents a relationship that must be satisfied *as a matter of conceptual fact*. It must obtain demonstrably on the basis of "general principles" if the truth-condition C is to qualify as adequate.

III. Truth as Ideal Coherence

Let us say that a factual proposition satisfies the condition of "ideal coherence" if it is optimally coherent with a perfected (or completed) data base. Given the nature of "coherence," such a proposition will fit more smoothly and consistently with this idealized data base than does its negation (and so consequently fits better than any other proposition that is incompatible with it). The ensuing discussion will establish that, *when ideal coherence is construed in this way, then truth is demonstrably tantamount to ideal coherence.* It will endeavor to make manifest the tight linkage between these two factors.

To establish this contention, it must be shown that two implication theses obtain with respect to any and all statements:

> (I) true → ideally coherent.

(II) ideally coherent → true.

The idea of "ideal coherence" operative here should be understood as being a matter of *optimal coherence* (coh) with a *perfected data base* (*B*). Deploying these abbreviations, it is clear that the two principles at issue can now be formulated in the following two implication theses:

(I) *S* is true → *S* COH *B*.

(II) *S* COH *B* → *S* is true.

Note that when the specific coherentist truth criterion stands in place of our earlier generic *C*, we have, by hypothesis, that *S* COH *B* is tantamount to $C(S/i(S))$. Accordingly, the two principles now at issue simply restate the continuity condition in the special case of a coherence criteriology of truth.

If the coherence theory is to be adequate, the validation of these two principles will be mandatory. They have to be grounded in the very nature of "optimal coherence (COH) with a perfected data base (*B*)." To establish them we shall need to look more closely at the crucial ideas at issue: the conceptions of "optimal coherence" and of a "perfected data base."

First a word about optimal coherence. Just what is it for a statement (*S*) to *cohere optimally* with a data base (*B*)? What does *S* COH *B* involve? The answer is provided by two conditions:

(1)   *S* is a member of some family of mutually exclusive and exhaustive alternatives: $\{S_1, S_2, S_3, \ldots, S_n\}$

(2)   *S* is more smoothly co-systematizable with *B* than is any of its rival alternatives S_j, singly or in combination. (Note that this means specifically that *S* is more smoothly co-systematizable with *B* than is not-*S*.)

To implement this second idea, we must have in hand some concrete principles of cognitive systematization for assessing the comparative extent to which a statement is consonant and coordinated with the information afforded by a group of others. However, since this is not the place for a full-scale presentation of a coherentist truth-criteriology, this issue is something which we shall here presuppose as a given.[27]

Let us now turn to the idea of a "perfected data base." Perfection has two components: *completeness* (or comprehensiveness) and *adequacy* (or definitiveness). These have the following ramifications:

(1)   *Completeness*: If D is to be a *perfected* data base, then it must be sufficiently complete and comprehensive that, for any thesis S within the domain of discussion at issue, either S itself or its negation not-S will cohere optimally with D:

> If perf (D), then: either S COH D or not-S COH D, for any and every statement S of the relevant domain.

(2)   *Adequacy*: To acknowledge D as a *perfected* data base is to acknowledge it as actuality-determinative. And so we must endorse:

> If perf (D), then: if S COH D, then $@(S)$, where $@$ is an actuality operator that so functions that $@(S) \rightarrow S$.

Completeness requires *decisiveness*; adequacy requires *facticity*. These are conditions that inhere in the very notion of the "perfection" of a data base.

To be sure, all this is not to say that we can ever actually *find* such a perfected data base. We doubtless cannot. The very idea of such a data base represents an idealization. The claim at issue is framed in a strictly hypothetical mode: "If a perfected data base exists, then it must *ipso facto* have the specified characteristics." We are, in effect, dealing with the *meaning postulates* or definitional requirements for the idea of a "perfected data base"—certain explanatory stipulations for what the idea of such a data base involves (in the context of "optimal coherence").

As a preliminary consideration, let us first establish the effective *uniqueness* of such a perfected data base in point of optimal coherence. To demonstrate this, let us make the assumption that both B_1 and B_2 answer to the characterization of a "perfected data base." We can then establish:

If S COH B_1, then S COH B_2, for any statement S.

This is accomplished by the following argument:

(1)   Suppose: S COH B_1

(2)   Suppose further that not-S COH B_2

(3)   Then not-S COH B_2 follows from (2) by Completeness

(4)   Then $@(\text{not-}S)$ follows from (3) by Adequacy

(5)   But $@(S)$ follows from (1) by Adequacy

(6)   Since (4) and (5) are mutually contradictory given the Law of the Excluded Middle, we must negate supposition (2), and hence have: S COH B_2. Q.E.D.

The converse of the preceding implication thesis also follows by exactly the same line of reasoning. And this shows that with respect to "optimal coherence" there is in effect (at most) one perfected data base. Let us continue to designate this by B. By definition, then, B is the (unique) perfected data base—whose availability, as already observed, we can claim not as a matter of realizable fact but only as a matter of idealization.

It follows immediately from the two stipulated requirements of Completeness and Adequacy that B must satisfy the conditions represented by the following principles:

(P1)   By the condition of Adequacy we have it that if S does indeed optimally cohere with B, then this state of affairs must be actual:

S COH $B \rightarrow @(S)$.

(P2)   By the condition of Completeness we have it that if S does not cohere optimally with the perfected data base (B), then it follows that not-S will be optimally coherent with the perfected data base B. Symbolically:

$(S$ COH $B) \rightarrow ($not-S COH $B)$.

These two principles, (P1) and (P2), will furnish the materials on whose basis our two focal implication theses (I) and (II) can and must be established. They are all we have; if the job is to be done, they must suffice to do it.

Before proceeding to show this, however, the idea of "factuality" reflected in our actuality-indicator $A(S)$ deserves some comment. The claim at issue is one of factuality, of "adequation to fact" (*adaequatio ad rem*): to assert $A(S)$ is to maintain that the state of affairs S is a constituent of the real world, that existing reality is (in part) characterized by this state of affairs. (Thus, to assert $A(S)$ is effectively to assert that S represents a "*bestehender Sachverhalt,*" an *actual state of affairs*, in the vocabulary of Ludwig Wittgenstein's *Tractatus Logico-Philosophicus*.) The thesis at issue with $A(S)$ is an *ontological* one: it claims that that is how things in fact are, whether or not people know or believe it. And this ontologically definitive aspect of A

means that we must have the "law of the excluded middle" represented by a *tertium non datur* principle:

(LEM) ~ $A(S)$ iff $A(\text{not-}S)$

Actuality must "make up its mind" with respect to the $A(S)$ vs. $A(\text{not-}S)$ dichotomy. This condition inheres axiomatically in the very meaning of "actuality."

On this basis, let us now proceed to establish principles (I) and (II) as stated on p. 19. The required demonstration is easily produced. Given that truth is (by definition, as it were) subject to the ancient principle of accord with fact (*adaequatio ad rem*):

(A) S is true $\leftrightarrow$ @(S)

we have it that principle (P1) immediately entails:

S COH $B \rightarrow S$ is true

This provides thesis II, so that half of our task is already accomplished.

To obtain thesis I, let us consider principle (P1) in the special case of the state of affairs not-S:

(1)~@(not-S) $\rightarrow$ ~(not-S COH B)

By the Law of Excluded Middle, namely:

(LEM) @(S) $\leftrightarrow$ ~@(not-S)

we have it that (1) yields:

(2)@(S) $\rightarrow$ ~(not-S COH B)

Now in view of (P2), this yields:

@(S) $\rightarrow$ S COH B

And given (A), this in turn yields:
      S is true $\rightarrow$ S COH B

We have thus also provided for thesis (I), thereby completing our task.

It follows from the resultant equivalence of truth-as-adequation on the one side with ideal coherence on the other that in adequationist view of the nature of truth affords no insuperable obstacles to coherentism. The co-ordinative linkage between truth and (idealized) coherence is grounded in the fundamental general principles of the matter, and the coherentist standard thus meets the crucial continuity condition that is an adequacy requirement for any viable criterion of truth. The continuity condition is satisfied. As regards its theoretical eligibility, we may inscribe *nihil obstat* on the proposal to construe truth in terms of idealized coherence.

IV. Coherentism and Truth as Adequation

It remains to be shown, however, that the "ancient principle of accord with fact, of *adaequatio ad rem*"—namely, thesis (A)—is also available to the coherentist who, after all, does not propose to *define* truth in this way, so that it is not to him a mere truism (as it is to the adequationist). Accordingly, we must show that this thesis is derivable on coherentist principles, given that these principles consist not of (P1) and (P2) alone, but also the favored truth-determinative axiom (or definition) that is obtained when we conjoin theses I and II:

(C) S is true $\leftrightarrow$ S COH B.

Note that in view of this axiom, we have it that (P1) yields

S is true $\rightarrow$ $A(S)$.

To obtain the converse, consider the principle (P1) in the special case of the state of affairs not-S:

$\sim@(\text{not-}S) \rightarrow \sim(\text{not-}S \text{ COH } B)$.

By the Law of Excluded Middle (LEM) this will entail:

$@(S) \rightarrow \sim(\text{not-}S \text{ COH } B)$.

By (P2) this yields:

$@(S) \rightarrow S$ COH B.

By (C) this yields:

$@(S) \rightarrow S$ is true.

Together with its converse, as derived above, this provides for (A). Q.E.D.

It follows that an equating of "the (real) truth" with adequation to fact (with how matters actually stand in the world) is also an implicit consequence—*in the idealized case*—of a coherentist conception of the nature of truth. The coherentist accordingly has no need to renounce adequation. In defining truth in terms of ideal coherence, the principle of adequation (A) remains available to the coherentist as reflecting an essential feature of truth. The idea that principle (A) characterizes the essence of truth is as available to him as to anyone else.

Let us recall that principle (A) encapsulates the *correspondentist* view of the nature of truth as truth-adequation to fact:

(A) S is true $\leftrightarrow$ @(S).

On the other hand, principle (C) encapsulates the *coherentist* view of the nature of truth as ideal coherence:

(C) S is true $\leftrightarrow$ S COH B.

The first stage of our argumentation has established:

{(LEM), (P1), (P2), (A)} entails (C).

And the second stage of our argumentation has established:

{(LEM), (P1), (P2), (C)} entails (A).

Putting these together, we arrive at:

{(LEM), (P1), (P2)} entails [(A) $\leftrightarrow$ (C)]

Given the explanation of "ideal coherence" at issue in the principles P1 and P2 (or, equivalently, the conditions of *Completeness* and *Adequacy*), it emerges that adequationism and coherentism are effectively co-ordinated. The coherentist criteriology of truth is also available to the adequationist. The adequationist view of the nature of truth is also available to the coherentist. The two positions can (under plausible suppositions) be co-ordinated with one another as deductively equivalent.

The salient problem of this chapter's first section is thus resolved. The present deliberations indicate that the coherentist criterion of truth as optimal systematization is qualified to serve as a truth-

criterion in virtue of satisfying the continuity condition. Authentic
truth may be characterized essentialistically in terms of *idealized* coherence; putative truth may be identified criteriologically in terms of
manifest coherence. And the requisite continuity between the two
conceptions is thus assured.

This is all to the good. Brand Blanshard's insistence on the continuity condition is very much in order. He urges, in effect, that "If you
are seriously proposing to adopt coherence with 'the data' as a crite-
rial standard of truth, then you should be able to show this proposal to
be warranted through some sort of essential linkage between truth and
coherence." As he puts it:

> If we accept coherence as our test, we must use it everywhere.
> We must therefore use it to test the suggestion that truth is other
> than coherence. But if we do, we shall find that we must reject the
> suggestion as leading to incoherence.[28]

And this point is well taken. A definition or interpretation of truth that
did not meet this condition would thereby manifest its own inadequacy. In showing that the coherentist criterion of truth is capable of
meeting the continuity condition, the present deliberations manage to
set aside one of the main traditional reservations about the acceptability of coherentism. But only its resort to idealization makes this possible. Seeing that (as noted at the start) truth is inherently an idealization concept, it is clear that any adequate account of its nature and
modus operandi will inevitably have to take this circumstance into
account.

V. The Gap Between The Real and The Ideal

To be sure, an important issue remains open. Given that "the real
truth" is guaranteed only by ideal coherence—by optimal coherence
with a perfected data base that we do not have, rather than by apparent coherence with the suboptimal data base we actually have in
hand—we have no categorical assurance of the actual correctness of
our coherence-guided inquiries. Nor do we have an unqualified guarantee that their deliverances provide "the real truth" that we seek in
matters of empirical inquiry. Quite the reverse. The history of science
shows that our "discoveries" about how things work in the world secured through scientific coherentism constantly require adjustment,
correction, and replacement. The history of science is a saga of ongoing changes and improvements—which means of changes of mind.
We cannot say that our coherence-grounded scientific theorizing pro-

vides us with the real (definitive) truth, but just that it provides us with the best estimate of the truth that we can achieve in the circumstances at hand.

An important point in epistemology thus lies at the core of our deliberations. The essential linkage between truth and rational justification is not definitional (we do not have it that: truth = justified belief). Nor again is this linkage an empirical matter of an observed statistical correlation: "our justified beliefs are true most of the time"—a contention which, in the case of natural science at any rate, is falsified rather than confirmed by the course of experience. Rather, the linkage between truth and rational justification is secured in the conceptual order, albeit only at the level of idealization: truth is rationally justified belief in ideal cases.

Definitive knowledge—as opposed to "merely putative" knowledge—is the fruit of perfected inquiry. Only here, at the idealized level of perfected science, could we count on securing the real truth about the world that "corresponds to reality" as the traditional phrase has it. And factual knowledge at the level of generality and precision at issue in scientific theorizing is akin to a perfect circle. Try as we will, we cannot quite succeed in producing it in actual practice. We do our best and call the result knowledge—even as we call that carefully drawn "circle" on the blackboard a circle. So here again the crucial difference between certifying truth-conditions and estimative use-conditions will have to come into play.

Of course we fully realize that what we currently call scientific knowledge is no more authentic (perfected) knowledge than what we call a circle in a geometry diagram is an authentic (perfected) circle. Our "knowledge" is in such cases no more than our best estimate of the idealization represented by "the actual truth of things." For there is not finding of the science of the day that does not admit of refinement and improvement. Lacking the advantage of a God's-eye view, we have no access to the world's facts save through the mediation of (potentially flawed) inquiry. All we can do—and what must suffice us because indeed it is all that we can do—is to do the best we can with the cognitive state of the art to estimate "the correct" answers to our scientific questions. Coherence as best we can realize it comes to stand surrogate for optimal coherence.

In the subideal, real-life conditions of an epistemically difficult world, an evidential gap indeed separates presumptive from certifiable truth. But given an adequate criteriology of truth, this gap becomes closed in ideal circumstances. The continuity condition reflects the fact that inquiry aims at truth—that the real truth is the definitive aim and aspiration of the scientific enterprise. The circumstance that what we achieve in our practice of cognitive coherentism is not the real truth as such, but only our best estimate, reflects the fact that we must pursue this cognitive enterprise amid the harsh realities and complexities of an imperfect world. In deliberating about the truth of our factual claims, as elsewhere, the gap between the real and the ideal must be acknowledged.

And so with truth as with ideals in general we face the tension inherent in two considerations: On the one hand we have to do with an idealization that is essential for communicative purposes but not readily evidentiated by the determinable facts. On the other hand we implement our recourse to this ideal by means of realistically realizable use conditions.

Moreover these deliberations regarding truth as idealized coherence convey a wider lesson. For they provide a vivid illustration of what might be called the Fundamental Principle of Idealization which is encapsulated in the following thesis:

> If conditions $C_1, C_2, \ldots C_n$ are those we *actually* use in determining that something is an X, then the idealization of these several conditions will thereby also serve to determine what it is to be an ideal X.

In sum: The idealized product stands correlative with the manifold of its idealized factors. To be an ideal X is to possess to an ideal (i.e., completed and perfected) extent those features that actual practice serve to determine something to be an X. This principle establishes a fundamental and indissoluble link between the make-up of the real and structure of the ideal.[29]

VI. Truth as an Idealization

Definitive truth is realizable only by way of idealization: actual inquiry presents us with *estimates* of truth, in matters of scientific theorizing, the real truth as such is realizable only under ideal conditions.

We have no alternative to presuming that *our* science as it stands here and now does not present the real truth, but only *estimates* it. "Our truth" in matters of scientific theorizing is not—and presumably never actually will be—the final truth. However confidently science may affirm its conclusions, the realization must be maintained that its declarations are provisional, tentative—subject to revision and even to outright abandonment and replacement. But all this is not, of course, any reason to abandon the link to truth at the teleological level of aims, goals and aspirations. The pursuit of scientific truth, like the pursuit of happiness, or for that matter any other ideal in life, is not vitiated by the consideration that its full realization is not a matter of the practicalities of this imperfect world.

The ideal of a state-of-the-art in science that attains definitive finality in empirical inquiry is pie in the sky. It represents an idealization and not a matter of the practical politics of the epistemic domain. But it affords the *focus imaginarius* whose pursuit canalizes and structures our actions. It represents the ultimate objective (goal) of inquiry—the destination of an incompletable journey. The conception of capital-T Truth thus serves a negative and fundamentally regulative role to mark the fact that the place we have attained falls short of our capacity actually to realize our cognitive aspirations. It marks a fundamental contrast that *regulates* how we do and must view our claims to have got at the truth of things. It plays a role somewhat reminiscent of the functionary who reminded the Roman emperor of his mortality in reminding us that our pretensions to truth are always vulnerable. Contemplation of this ideal enables us to maintain the ever-renewed recognition of the essential ambiguity of the human condition as suspended between the reality of imperfect achievement and the ideal of an unattainable perfection.

We must suppose that science does not and cannot attain an omega-condition of final perfection. The prospect of fundamental changes lying just around the corner can never be eliminated finally and decisively.

A basic analogy obtains as per the following proposition:

putative knowledge: actual inquiry: genuine knowledge: ideal inquiry

Rational inquiry is the pursuit of an unattainable ideal—the ideal of "the real truth" about laws of nature as yielded by perfected science. Actual inquiry is no more than our best effort in this direction, and the information (the putative knowledge) it yields is no more than our best available *estimate* of the real truth of things.

To abandon this conception of the truth as such—rejecting the idea of an "ideal science" which alone can properly be claimed to afford a grasp of reality—would be to abandon an idea which crucially regulates our view as to the nature and status of the knowledge we lay claim to. We would then no longer be constrained to characterize our truth as *merely* ostensible and purported. And then, did our truth not exhibit any blatant *inherent* imperfections, we would be tempted to view it as real, authentic and final in a manner which as we at bottom realize it does not deserve.

The lesson of these deliberations is clear. What we have in view in speaking of "the real truth" in scientific matters is not the actual product of current inquiry, but the hypothesized product of idealized inquiry. The conditions of objectivity and definitiveness we have in view in relation to "the real truth" are not satisfiable in the circumstances in which we do and unavoidably must labor. In this regard we have no realistic alternative but to regard the truth in these matters as having an idealization.

Conceptions such as definitive knowledge and truth in matters of scientific theorizing are idealizations geared to the idea of completed and perfected science. And this—all too obviously—is not something we have in hand. It is no more than a regulative ideal that guides and directs our efforts in question-resolving inquiry.

Such an ideal is not (or should not be) something that is unhealthily unrealistic. It should produce not defeatism and negativity towards our efforts and their fruits but rather a positive determination to do yet better and fill a half-full barrel yet fuller. It should represent not our expectations of realized achievement but our aspirations, and should govern not our demands but our hopes. Endowing us with a healthy scepticism towards what we actually have in hand, it should encourage our determination to further improvements and should act not as an obstacle but a goal.

And here, as elsewhere, we must reckon appropriately with the standard gap between aspiration and attainment. In the practical sphere—in craftmanship, for example, or the cultivation of our health—we may *strive* for perfection, but cannot ever claim to *attain* it. And the situation in inquiry is exactly parallel with what we encounter in such other domains—ethics specifically included. The value of an ideal, even of one that is not realizable, lies not in the benefit of its attainment (obviously and *ex hypothesi*!) but in the benefits that accrue from its pursuit. The view that it is rational to pursue an aim only if we are in a position to achieve its attainment or approximation is mistaken; it can be perfectly valid (and entirely rational) if the indirect benefits of its pursuit and adoption are sufficient—if in striving after it, we realize relevant advantages to a substantial degree. An unattainable ideal can be enormously productive. And so, the legitimation of the ideas of "perfected science" lies in its facilitation of the ongoing evolution of inquiry. In this domain, we arrive at the perhaps odd-seeming posture of an invocation of practical utility for the validation of an ideal.

CHAPTER FIVE

ON IDEAL SCIENCE AND THE
INFEASIBILITY OF ITS REALIZATION

I. The Problem of Completion

How far can the scientific enterprise advance toward a definitive understanding of reality? Might science attain a point of recognizable completion? Is the achievement of perfected science a genuine possibility, even in theory when all of the "merely practical" obstacles are put aside as somehow incidental?

What would *perfected science* be like? What sort of standards would it have to meet? Clearly, it would have to complete in full the discharge of natural science's mandate or mission. Now, the goal-structure of scientific inquiry covers a good deal of ground. It is diversified and complex, spreading across both the cognitive/theoretical and active/practical sectors. It encompasses the traditional quartet of description, explanation, prediction, and control, in line with the following picture:

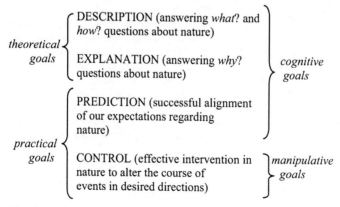

The theoretical sector concerns itself with matters of characterizing, explaining, accounting for, and rendering intelligible—with purely intellectual and informative issues, in short. By contrast, the practical sector is concerned with guiding actions, canalizing expectations, and, in general, with achieving the control over our environment that is required for the satisfactory conduct of our affairs. The former sector thus deals with what science enables us to *say*, and the latter with what it enables us to *do*. The one relates to our role as spectators of nature, the other to our role as active participants.

It thus appears that if we are to claim that our science has attained a perfected condition, it would have to satisfy (at least) the four following conditions:

1. *Erotetic completeness*: It must answer, in principle at any rate, all those descriptive and explanatory questions that it itself countenances as legitimately raisable, and must accordingly explain everything it deems explicable.

2. *Predictive completeness*: It must provide the cognitive basis for accurately predicting those eventuations that are in principle predictable (that is, those which it itself recognizes as such).

3. *Pragmatic completeness*: It must provide the requisite cognitive means for doing whatever is feasible for beings like ourselves to do in the circumstances in which we labor.

4. *Temporal finality* (the omega-condition): It must leave no room for expecting further substantial changes that destabilize the existing state of scientific knowledge.

Each of these modes of substantive completeness deserves detailed consideration. First, however, one brief preliminary remark. It is clear that any condition of science that might qualify as "perfected" would have to meet certain formal requirements of systemic unity. If, for example, there are different routes to one and the same question (for instance, if both astronomy and geology can inform us about the age of the earth), then these answers will certainly have to be consistent. Perfected science will have to meet certain requirements of structural systematicity in the manner of its articulation: it must be coherent, consistent, consonant, uniform, harmonious, and so on. Such requirements represent purely formal cognitive demands upon the architectonic of articulation of a body of science that could lay any claim to perfection. Interesting and important though they are, we shall not, however, trouble about these *formal* requirements here, our present concern being with various *substantive* issues.[30]

II. Theoretical Adequacy: Issues of Erotetic Completeness

Erotetic completeness is an unattainable mirage. We can never exhaust the possibility of questions. The Kantian Principle of question propagation means that inquiry—the dialectic of questions and answers—can never get to the ultimate bottom of things.

Any adequate theory of inquiry must recognize that the ongoing process of science is a process of *conceptual* innovation that always leaves certain theses wholly outside the cognitive range of the inquirers of any particular period. This means that there will always be facts (or plausible candidate-facts) about a thing that we do not *know* because we cannot even conceive of them. For to grasp such a fact calls for taking a perspective of consideration that we simply do not have, since the state of knowledge (or purported knowledge) is not yet advanced to a point at which its entertainment is feasible. In bringing conceptual innovation about, cognitive progress makes it possible to consider new possibilities that were heretofore conceptually inaccessible.

The language of emergence can perhaps be deployed profitably to make the point. But what is at issue is not an emergence of *the features of things* but an emergence in our *knowledge* about them. The blood circulated in the human body well before Harvey; uranium-containing substances were radioactive before Becquerel. The emergence at issue relates to our cognitive mechanisms of conceptualization, not to the objects of our consideration in and of themselves. Real-world objects are conceived of as antecedent to any cognitive interaction—as being there right along, or "pregiven," as Edmund Husserl puts it. Any cognitive changes or innovations are to be conceptualized as something that occurs on our side of the cognitive transaction, and not on the side of the objects with which we deal.[31]

And the prospect of change can never be dismissed in this domain. The properties of a thing are literally open-ended: we can always discover more of them. Even if we view the world as inherently finitistic, and espouse a Principle of Limited Variety which has it that nature can be portrayed descriptively with the materials of a finite taxonomic scheme, there can be no *a priori* guarantee that the progress of science will not engender an unending sequence of changes of mind regarding this finite register of descriptive materials. And this conforms exactly to our expectation in these matters. For where the real things of the world are concerned, we not only expect to learn more about them in the course of scientific inquiry, *we expect to have to change our mind about their nature and mode of comportment.* Be it elm trees, or volcanoes, or quarks that are at issue, we have every expectation that in the course of future scientific progress people will come to think differently about them than we ourselves do at this juncture.

Cognitive inexhaustibility thus emerges as a definitive feature of our conception of a real thing. In claiming knowledge about such things, we are always aware that the object transcends what we know about it—that yet further and different facts concerning it can always come to light, and that all that we *do* say about it does not exhaust all that *can* be said about it.

The world's furnishings are cognitively opaque; we cannot see to the bottom of them. Knowledge can become more extensive without thereby becoming more complete. And this view of the situation is rather supported than impeded if we abandon a cumulativist/preservationist view of knowledge or purported knowledge for the view that new discoveries need not supplement but can displace old ones.

The concept of a thing so functions in our conceptual scheme that things are thought of as having an identity, a nature, and a mode of comportment wholly indifferent to the cognitive state-of-the-art regarding them, and presumably very different from our conceptions of the matter. But this is something we presume or postulate; it is certainly not something we have discovered—or ever could discover. We are not—and will never be—in a position to evade or abolish the contrast between "things as we think them to be" and "things as they actually and truly are." Their susceptibility to further elaborative detail-and to changes of mind regarding this further detail—is built into our very conception of a "real thing." To be a real thing is to be something regarding which we can always in principle acquire more information.

And much the same story holds when our concern is not with things but with *types* of things. To say that something is copper (or is magnetic) is to say more than that it has the properties we associate with copper (or magnetic things), and indeed is to say more than that it meets our test-conditions for being copper (or being magnetic). It is to say that this thing *is* copper (or magnetic). And this is an issue regarding which we are prepared at least to contemplate the prospect that we've got it wrong.

There is thus good reason of general principle to think that erotetic completeness is unachievable. But another line of consideration is no less decisive for our present purposes.

Could we ever actually achieve erotetic completeness (Q-completeness)—the condition of being able to resolve, in principle, all of our (legitimately posable) questions about the world? Could we ever find ourselves in this position?[32]

In theory, yes. A body of science certainly could be such as to provide answers to all those questions it allows to arise. But just how meaningful would this mode of completeness be?

It is sobering to realize that the erotetic completeness of a state of science S does not necessarily betoken its comprehensiveness or sufficiency. It might reflect the paucity of the range of questions we are prepared to contemplate—a deficiency of imagination, so to speak. When the range of our knowledge is sufficiently restricted, then its Q-completeness will merely reflect this impoverishment rather than its intrinsic adequacy. Conceivably, if improbably, science might reach a purely fortuitous equilibrium between problems and solutions. It could eventually be "completed" in the narrow erotetic sense—providing an answer to every question one can also in the then-existing (albeit still imperfect) state of knowledge—without thereby being completed in the larger sense of answering the questions that would arise if only one could probe nature just a bit more deeply. And so, our corpus of scientific knowledge could be erotetically complete and yet fundamentally inadequate. Thus, even if realized, this erotetic mode of completeness would not be particularly meaningful. (To be sure, this discussion proceeds at the level of supposition contrary to fact. The exfoliation of new questions from old in the course of scientific inquiry that is at issue in Kant's Principle of question-propagation spells the infeasibility of ever attaining Q-completeness.)

The preceding considerations illustrate a more general circumstance. Any claim to the realization of a *theoretically* complete science of physics would be one that affords "a complete, consistent, and unified theory of physical interaction that would describe all possible observations."[33] But to check that the state of physics on hand actually meets this condition, we would need to know exactly what physical interactions are indeed *possible*. And to warrant us in using the state of physics on hand as a basis for answering *this* question, we would *already* have to be assured that its view of the possibilities is correct—and thus already have preestablished its completeness. The idea of a consolidated erotetic completeness shipwrecks on the infeasibility of finding a meaningful way to monitor its attainment.

After all, any judgment we can make about the laws of nature—any model we can contrive regarding how things work in the world—is a matter of theoretical triangulation from the data at our disposal. And we should never have unalloyed confidence in the definitiveness of our data base or in the adequacy of our exploitation of it. Observation can never settle decisively just what the laws of nature are. In principle, different law-systems can always yield the same observational output: as philosophers of science want to insist, observations *underdetermine* laws. To be sure, this worries working scientists less

than philosophers, because they deploy powerful regulative principles—simplicity, economy, uniformity, homogeneity, and so on—to
constrain uniqueness. But neither these principles themselves nor the
uses to which they are put are unproblematic. No matter how comprehensive our data or how great our confidence in the inductions we
base upon them, the potential inadequacy of our claims cannot be
averted. One can never feel secure in writing *finis* on the basis of
purely theoretical considerations.

We can reliably estimate the amount of gold or oil yet to be
discovered, because we know *a priori* the earth's extent and can thus
establish a proportion between what we know and what we do not.
But we cannot comparably estimate the amount of knowledge yet to
be discovered, because we have and can have no way of relating what
we know to what we do not. At best, we can consider the proportion
of available questions we can in fact resolve; and this is an unsatisfac-
tory procedure (see pp. 38–39). The very idea of cognitive limits has
a paradoxical air. It suggests that we claim knowledge about something outside knowledge. But (to hark back to Hegel), with respect to
the realm of knowledge, we are not in a position to draw a line between what lies inside and what lies outside—seeing that, *ex hypothesi* we have no cognitive access to that latter. One cannot make a
survey of the relative extent of knowledge or ignorance about nature
except by basing it on some picture of nature that is already in hand—
that is, unless one is prepared to take at face value the deliverances of
existing science. This process of judging the adequacy of our science
on its own telling is the best we can do, but it remains an essentially
circular and consequently inconclusive way of proceeding. The long
and short of it is that there is no cognitively adequate basis for maintaining the completeness of science in a rationally satisfactory way.

To monitor the theoretical completeness of science, we accordingly need some theory-external control on the adequacy of our theorizing, some theory-external reality-principle to serve as a standard of
adequacy. We are thus driven to abandoning the road of pure theory
and proceeding along that of the practical goals of the enterprise. This
gives special importance and urgency to the pragmatic sector.

III. Pragmatic Completeness

The arbitrament of praxis—not theoretical merit but practical capability—affords the best standard of adequacy for our scientific proceed-
ings that is available. But could we ever be in a position to claim that
science has been completed on the basis of the success of its practical
applications? On this basis, the perfection of science would have to

manifest itself in the perfecting of control—in achieving a perfected technology. But just how are we to proceed here? Could our natural science achieve manifest perfection on the side of control over nature? Could it ever underwrite a recognizably perfected technology?

The issue of "control over nature" involves much more complexity than may appear on first view. For just how is this conception to be understood? Clearly, in terms of bending the course of events to our will, of attaining our ends within nature. But this involvement of *"our ends"* brings to light the prominence of our own contribution. For example, if we are inordinately modest in our demands (or very unimaginative), we may even achieve "complete control over nature" in the sense of being in a position to do *whatever we want* to do, but yet attain this happy condition in a way that betokens very little real capability.

One might, to be sure, involve the idea of omnipotence, and construe a "perfected" technology as one that would enable us to do literally *anything*. But this approach would at once run into the old difficulties already familiar to the medieval scholastics. They were faced with the challenge: "If God is omnipotent, can he annihilate himself (contra his nature as a *necessary* being), or can he do evil deeds (contra his nature as a *perfect* being), or can he make triangles have four angles (contrary to *their* definitive nature)?" Sensibly enough, the scholastics inclined to solve these difficulties by maintaining that an omnipotent God need not be in a position to do literally anything but rather simply anything which it *is possible* for him to do. Similarly, we cannot explicate the idea of technological omnipotence in terms of a capacity to produce and result, wholly without qualification. We cannot ask for the production of a *perpetuum mobile*, for spaceships with "hyperdrive" enabling them to attain transluminar velocities, for devices that predict essentially stochastic processes such as the disintegrations of transuranic atoms, or for piston devices that enable us to set *independently* the values for the pressure, temperature, and volume of a body of gas. We cannot, in sum, as of a "perfected" technology that it should enable us to do anything that we might take it into our heads to do, no matter how "unrealistic" this might be.

All that we can reasonably ask of it is that perfected technology should enable us to do anything *that it is possible for us to do*—and not just what we might *think* we can do but what we really and truly *can* do. A perfected technology would be one that enabled us to do anything that *can possibly* be done by creatures circumstanced as we are. But how can we deal with the pivotal conception of "can" that is at issue here? Clearly, only science—real, true, correct, *perfected* science—could tell us what indeed is realistically possible and what circumstances are indeed inescapable. Whenever our "knowledge"

falls short of this, we may well "ask the impossible" by way of accomplishment (for example, spaceships in "hyperdrive"), and thus
complain of incapacity to achieve control in ways that put unfair bur-
dens on this conception.

Power is a matter of the "effecting of things possible"—of
achieving control—and it is clearly cognitive state-of-the-art in science which, in teaching us about the limits of the possible, is itself the
agent that must shape our conception of this issue. *Every* law of nature serves to set the boundary between what is genuinely possible
and what is not, between what can be done and what cannot, between
which questions we can properly ask and which we cannot. We cannot satisfactorily monitor the adequacy and completeness of our science by its ability to effect "all things possible," because science
alone can inform us about what is possible. As science grows and
develops, it poses new issues of power and control, reformulating and
reshaping those demands whose realization represents "control over
nature." For science itself brings new possibilities to light. (At a suitable stage, the idea of "splitting the atom" will no longer seem a con-
tradiction in terms.) To see if a given state of technology meets the
condition of perfection, we must *already* have a body of perfected
science in hand to tell us what is indeed possible. To validate the
claim that our technology is perfected, we need to *preestablish* the
completeness of our science. The idea works in such a way that
claims to perfected control can rest only on perfected science.

In attempting to travel the practicalist route to cognitive completeness, we are thus trapped in a circle. Short of having supposedly
perfected science in hand, we could not say what a perfected technology would be like, and thus we could not possibly monitor the perfection of science in terms of the technology that it underwrites.

Moreover, even if (*per impossible*) a "pragmatic equilibrium"
between what we can and what we wish to do in science were to be
realized, we could not be warrantedly confident that this condition
will remain unchanged. The possibility that "just around the corner
things will become unstuck can never be eliminated. Even if we
"achieve control" to all intents and purposes, we cannot be sure of not
losing our grip upon it—not because of a loss of power but because of
cognitive changes that produce a broadening of the imagination and a
widened apprehension as to what "having control" involves.

Accordingly, the project of achieving practical mastery can never
be perfected in a satisfactory way, The point is that control hinges on
what we want, and what we want is conditioned by what we think
possible, and *this* is something that hinges crucially on theory—on
our beliefs about how things work in this world. And so control is
something deeply theory-infected. We can never safely move from

apparent to real adequacy in this regard. We cannot adequately assure that seeming perfection is more than just that. We thus have no alternative but to *presume* that our knowledge (that is, our purported knowledge) is inadequate at this and indeed at any other particular stage of the game of cognitive completeness.

One important point about control must, however, be noted with care. Our preceding negative strictures all relate to attainment of perfect control—of being in a position to do everything possible. No such problems affect the issue of amelioration—of doing some things better and *improving* our control over what it was. It makes perfectly good sense to use its technological applications as standards of scientific advancement. (Indeed, we have no real alternative to using pragmatic standards at this level, because reliance on theory alone is, in the end, going to be circular.) While control does not help us with *perfection*, it is crucial for monitoring *progress*. Standards of assessment and evaluation are such that we can implement the idea of improvements (progress), but not that of completion (realized perfection). We can determine when we have managed to *enlarge* our technological mastery, but we cannot meaningfully say what it would be to *perfect* it. (Our conception of the *doable* keeps changing with changes in the cognitive state-of-the-art, a fact that does not, of course, alter our view of what *already has been done* in the practical sphere.)

With regard to technical perfectibility, we must recognize that (1) there is no reason to expect that its realization is possible, even in principle, and (2) it is not monitorable: even if we had achieved it, we would not be able to claim success with warranted confidence. In the final analysis, then, we cannot regard the *realization* of "completed science" as a meaningful prospect—we cannot really say what it is that we are asking for. (To be sure, what is meaningless here is not the idea of perfected science as such but the idea of *achieving* it.) There deliberations further substantiate the idea that we must always presume our knowledge to be incomplete in the domain of natural science.

IV. Predictive Completeness

The difficulties encountered in using physical control as a standard of "perfection" in science all also hold with respect to *prediction*, which, after all, is simply a mode of *cognitive* control.

Suppose someone asks: "Are you really still going to persist in plaints regarding the incompleteness of scientific knowledge when science can predict *everything*?" The reply is simply that science will *never* be able to predict literally everything: the very idea of predicting *everything* is simply unworkable. For then, whenever we predict something, we would have to predict also the effects of making those predictions, and then the ramification of *those* predictions, and so on *ad indefinitum*. The very most that can be asked is that science put us into a position to predict, not *everything*, but rather *anything* that we might choose to be interested in and to inquire about. And here it must be recognized that our imaginative perception of the possibilities might be much too narrow. We can only make predictions about matters that lie, at least broadly speaking, within our cognitive horizons. Newton could not have predicted findings in quantum theory any more than he could have predicted the outcome of American presidential elections. One can only make predictions about what one is cognizant of, takes note of, deems worthy of consideration. In this regard, one can be myopic either by not noting or by losing sight of significant sectors of natural phenomena.

Another important point must be made regarding this matter of unpredictability. Great care must be taken to distinguish the ontological and the epistemological dimensions, to keep the entries of these two columns apart:

unexplainable	not (yet) explained
by chance	by some cause we do not know of
spontaneous	caused in a way we cannot identify
random	lawful in ways we cannot characterize
by whim	for reasons not apparent to us

It is tempting to slide from epistemic incapacity to ontological lawfulness. But we must resist this temptation and distinguish what is inherently uncognizable from what we just don't happen to cognize. The nature of scientific change makes it inevitably problematic to slide from present to future incapacity.

Sometimes, to be sure, talk in the ontological mode is indeed warranted. The world no doubt contains situations of randomness and chance, situations in which genuinely stochastic processes are at work in a ways that "engenders unknowability." But these ontological claims must root in knowledge rather than ignorance. They can only be claimed appropriately in those cases in which (as in quantum theory) *we can explain inexplicability*—that is, in which we can account for the inability to predict/explain/control within the framework of a positive account of why the item at issue is actually unpredictable/unexplainable/unsolvable.

Accordingly, these ontological based incapacities do *not* introduce matters that "lie beyond the limits of knowledge." On the contrary, positive information is the pivot point. the only viable limits to knowability are those which root in knowledge—that is, in a model of nature which entails that certain sorts of things are unknowable. It is not a matter of an incapacity to answer appropriate questions ("We 'just don't know' why that stochastic process eventuated as it did"). Rather, in the prevailing state of knowledge, these questions are improper; they just do not arise.

Science itself sets the limits to predictability—insisting that some phenomena (the stochastic processes encountered in quantum physics, for example) are inherently unpredictable. And this is always to some degree problematic. The most that science can reasonably be asked to do is to predict what it itself sees as in principle predictable—to answer every predictive question that it itself countenances as proper. And here we must once more recognize that any given state of science might have gotten matters quite wrong.

With regard to predictions, we are thus in the same position that obtains with regard to actually interventionist (rather than "merely cognitive") control. Here, too, we can unproblematically apply the idea of improvement—of progress. But it makes no sense to contemplate the *achievement* of perfection. For its realization is something we could never establish by any practicable means.

V. Temporal Finality

Scientists from time to time indulge in eschatological musings and tell us that the scientific venture is approaching its end.[34] And it is, of course, entirely *conceivable* that natural science will come to a stop, and will do so not in consequence of a cessation of intelligent life but in C. S. Peirce's more interesting sense of completion of the project: of eventually reaching a condition after which even indefinitely ongoing inquiry will not—and indeed in the very nature of things *cannot*—produce any significant change, because inquiry has come to "the end of the road." The situation would be analogous to that envisaged in the apocryphal story in vogue during the middle 1800s regarding the Commissioner of the United States Patents who resigned his post because there was nothing left to invent.[35]

Such a position is in theory possible. But here, too, we can never determine that it is actual.

There is no practicable way in which the claim that science has achieved temporal finality can be validated. The question "Is the current state of science, *S*, final?" is one for which we can never legitimate an affirmative answer. For the prospect of future changes of *S* can never be precluded. One cannot plausibly move beyond "We have (in S) no good reason to think that S will ever change" to obtain "We have (in S) good reason to think that S will never change." To take this posture towards S is to *presuppose its completeness.*[36] It is not simply to take the natural and relatively unproblematic stance that that for which S vouches is to be taken as true but to go beyond this to insist that whatever is true finds a rationalization within S. This argument accordingly embeds *finality* in *completeness*, and in doing so jumps from the frying pan into the fire. For it shifts from what is difficult to what is yet more so. To hold that if something is so at all, then S affords a good reason for it is to take so blatantly ambitious (even megalomaniacal) a view of S that the issue of finality seems almost a harmless appendage.

Moreover, just as the appearance of erotetic and pragmatic equilibrium can be a product of narrowness and weakness, so can temporal finality. We may think that science is unchangeable simply because we have been unable to change it. But that's just not good enough. Were science ever to come to a seeming stop, we could never be sure that is had done so not because it is at "the end of the road" but because we are at the end of our tether. We can never ascertain that science has attained the ω-condition of final completion, since from our point of view the possibility of further change lying "just around the corner" can never be ruled out finally and decisively. No matter how final a position we *appear* to have reached, the prospects of its coming unstuck cannot be precluded. As we have seen, future science is inscrutable. We can never claim with assurance that the position we espouse in immune to change under the impact of further data—that the oscillations are dying out and we are approaching a final limit. In its very nature, science "in the limit" related to what happens in the long run, and this is something about which we *in principle* cannot gather information: any information we can actually gather inevitably pertains to the short run and not the long run. We can never achieve adequate assurance that *apparent* definitiveness is *real*. We can never consolidate the claim that science has settled into a frozen, changeless pattern. The situation in natural science is such that our knowledge of nature must ever be presumed to be incomplete.

The idea of achieving a state of recognizably completed science is totally unrealistic. Even as widely variant modes of behavior by three dimensional objects could produce exactly the same two-dimensional shadow-projections, so very different law-systems could in principle engender exactly the same phenomena. We cannot make any definitive inferences from phenomena to the nature of the real. The prospect of perfected science is bound to elude us.

One is thus brought back to the stance of the great Idealist philosophers (Plato, Spinoza, Hegel, Bradley, Royce) that human knowledge inevitably falls short of recognizably "perfected science" (the Ideas, the Absolute), and must accordingly be looked upon as incomplete.

We have no alternative but to proceed on the assumption that the era of innovation is not over—that *future* science can and will prove to be *different* science.

As these deliberations indicate, the conditions of perfected science in point of description, explanation, prediction, and control are all unrealizable. Our information will inevitably prove inconclusive. We have no reasonable alternative to seeing our present-day science as suboptimal, regardless of the question of what date the calendar shows.

Note that the present discussion does not propound the *ontological* theses that natural science cannot be pragmatically complete, ω-definitive, and so on, but the *epistemological* thesis that science cannot ever be *known to be so*. The point is not that the requirements of definitive knowledge cannot in the nature of things be satisfied but that they cannot be *implemented* (that is, be *shown* to be satisfied). The upshot is that science must always be presumed to be incomplete, not that it necessarily always is so. No doubt this is also true. It cannot, however, be demonstrated on the basis of epistemological general principles but requires the substantive considerations.

VI. Science and Idealization

The fact that what we actually achieve in theorizing inquiry is not the real truth as such, but only our best realizable *estimate* of it, means that we must pursue this cognitive enterprise amid the harsh realities and complexities of an imperfect world. In deliberating about the truth of our scientific claims, as elsewhere, the gap between the real and the ideal must unavoidably be acknowledged. In the subideal, real-life conditions of an epistemically difficult world, an evidential gap indeed separates *presumptive* from *certifiable* truth. But given an adequate criteriology of truth, this gap becomes closed in ideal circumstances. The continuity condition reflects the fact that inquiry aims at truth—that the real truth is the definitive aim and aspiration of the scientific enterprise.

Given "the facts of life" in empirical inquiry, we have neither the inclination nor the justification to claim that the world is as our *present* science describes it to be. Nor, as we have seen, does it make sense to identify "the real truth" with "the truth as science-in-the-limit will eventually see it to be." All that can be done in this direction is to say that the world exists as *ideal or perfected* science describes it to be. The real, which is to say, final and definitive truth about nature at the level of scientific generality and precision is something we certainly cannot assume to be captured by *our* science as it stands here and now (thought, of course, this fact nowise destroys the rationality of our endorsement of current beliefs). We cannot but take the stance that scientific truth is not something in hand, but something which—so we must suppose—is attained only in the ideal or perfected state of things. With respect to scientific issues we thus arrive at the coordinating equation:

the real truth = the truth as ideal (perfected) science purports it to be

To be sure, in espousing this conception, we intend to make "ideal science" contingent upon truth, rather than the reverse: the former is the independent, the latter the dependent variable.

While one can never lay claim to have definitely secured "the real truth" in matters of scientific theorizing, this notion nevertheless serves an important role in providing a contrast-conception that constitutes a useful reminder of the fragility of our cognitive endeavors. It establishes a contrast between *our* present science as we have it and a perfected "ideal science" which alone can properly be claimed to afford a grasp of reality, an idea which crucially regulates our view as to the nature and status of the knowledge we lay claim to and thereby productively fosters the conduct of inquiry.

Such a recourse to ideal science is unavoidable. In the practical sphere—in craftsmanship, for example, or the cultivation of our health—we may *strive* for perfection, but cannot ever claim to have *attained* it, a situation that we also encounter in other domains—ethics specifically included. And the situation in inquiry is no different. The value of a *telos* need not necessarily inhere in the benefit of its attainment can also reside in the benefits that accrue from its pursuit. The view that it is rational to pursue a goal only if we are in a position to achieve its attainment or approximation is mistaken. The goal can be perfectly valid, and entirely rational, if the indirect benefits of its pursuit and adoption are sufficient—if in striving after it we realize relevant advantages in substantial degree. An unattainable ideal can be enormously productive.

But what of the objection that we could not tell that we had arrived at "the definitive truth" even if we in fact had done so? Its resolution lies in the fact that the attainment of such an objective is simply not at issue.

The goal of monitoring the correctness of our science independently of mind so to speak externally from its own efforts is clearly infeasible in principle. In this imperfect epistemic dispensation, we have to reckon with the realities of the human condition. In science as in other domains of human endeavor, it is a matter of doing the best we can with the tools that come to hand. We can pursue a goal in the full realization that perfection is unattainable in its achievement.

But the unattainability of *perfection* does nothing to countervail against the no less real fact that *improvement* is realizable—that progress is possible. The undeniable prospect of realizable progress—of overcoming genuine defects and deficiencies that we find in the work of our predecessors—affords ample impetus to scientific innovation. The labors of science are not pulled forward by the mirage of (unattainable) perfection. We are pushed onward by the (perfectly realizable) wish to do better than our predecessors in the enterprise.

We can understand "progress" in two senses. On the one hand, there is O-progress, defined in terms of increasing distance from the starting point (the "origin"). On the other hand, there is D-progress, defined in terms of decreasing distance from the goal (the "destination.") Consider the picture:

Origin   destination

O the attained position D

Ordinarily, the two modes of progress are entirely equivalent: we increase the distance traveled from O by exactly the same amount as we decrease the distance remaining to D. But if there is no attainable destination—if we are engaged on a journey that, for all we know, is literally endless and has no determinable destination, or only one that is "infinitely distant"—then we just cannot manage to decrease our distance from it.

Given that in natural science we are embarked on a journey that is literally endless, it is only O-progress that can be achieved, and not D-progress. We can gauge our progress only in terms of how far we have come by way of imposing upon our ventures in prediction and control, and not in terms of how far we have to go. Embarked on a journey that is in principle endless, we simply cannot say that we are nearing the goal.

The upshot is straightforward. The idea of *improving* our science can be implemented without difficulty, since we can clearly improve our performance as regards its practical tasks of prediction, control, and the rest. But the idea of *perfecting* our science in terms of its theoretical adequacy and accuracy cannot be implemented. And no harm results from conceding this. Nor does it destroy the utility of the idea of perfected science.

Perfected science—and the definitive truth that it affords us—is an ideal, and an ideal is not something we encounter in experience, but rather the hypothetical projection or extrapolation of what we encounter in experience. And the legitimacy of our cognitive ideals as regulators inhere in their *utility* as guides to inquiry, and specifically in their capacity to guide our thoughts and efforts in constructive and productive directions. It is a fallacy to see the validity of goals and ideals to reside solely and wholly in the presumed consequence of their *realization*. The benefits may reside not in arriving but in the pursuing itself. The striving after an ideal science that affords us "the ultimate truth" about the workings of nature seems to be a *telos* of just this sort. Its legitimation lies in its facilitation of the ongoing evolution of inquiry. In this domain, we arrive once again at the perhaps odd-seeming posture of an invocation of practical utility for the validation of ideal.[37]

The ideal status of "the truth" in scientific matters carries wider implications for how we can and should regard the actual deliverances of natural science. A salient example of this is the conception of a "natural law" which lies at the very core of our conception of nature. By definition, a "natural law" is "a genuine truth regarding some universal feature of the workings of nature." But insofar as, from the cognitive point of view, truth and universality are idealizations, so also is lawfulness, and with it such matters as space, time, element and the other conceptual building blocks of our understanding of nature.[38]

But ideal science is not something we have in hand here and now. And it is emphatically not something towards which we are moving along the asymptotic and approximative line envisaged by Peirce.[39] The asymptotic theory of scientific truth runs together two things that are by no means necessarily connected: there is in fact no warrant for identifying *ideal* or perfected science with *ultimate* science—science-in-the-limit. Even if it made sense to contemplate the Peircean idea of an eventual completion of science, there would be no guarantee that this completed science (given its existence) would satisfy the definitive requirements of a *perfected* science—would, for example, achieve the completeness of erotetic equilibrium where every posable question is duly resolved. Peircean convergentism is geared to the supposition that ultimate science—the science of the very distant future—will somehow prove to be an ideal of perfected science freed from the sorts of imperfections that afflict its predecessors. But the potential gap that arises here can only be closed by old-style, substantive metaphysics of a most problematic sort.

Perfected science is not something that exists here and how, nor is it something that lies ahead at some eventual offing in the remote future. It is not a real thing to be met with in this world. It is an idealization that exists "outside time"—that is, which cannot actually come to realization at all. It lies outside history as a useful contrast-case that cannot be numbered among the achieved realities of this imperfect world. Existing science does not and presumably never will embody to perfection cognitive ideals of completeness, unity, consistency, etc. These factors represent an aspiration rather than a coming reality: a *telos*, not a realizable condition of things—a hypothetical condition from which any and all of the negatives of the realized actual positions have been removed.

The concept of science perfected—of an ideal and completed science that captures the real truth of things and satisifies all of our cognitive ideals (definitiveness, completeness, unity, consistency, etc.)—is at best a useful fiction, a creature of the fictive imagination and not the secured product of inquiring reason. This "ideal science" is, as the very name suggests, an idealization, something that involves the removal in thought of limitations that obtain in fact. It involves the use of mind to move from a concern with the order of things as they are into the order of things as they ought to be.

VII. Actual Sciences as a Surrogate

While ideal science lies beyond our grasp, the fact remains that science as we actually have it represents our best-available estimate of its nature. Ideal science serves us as what Kant was wont to characterize as a *regulative ideal*, an imagined or envisioned *telos* whose conception provides us with an idealized modal of the goal at which our scientific endeavors should aim. It serves to orient our view of the scientific project in enabling us to see how values like truth and importance should and would operate if everything went as its ideally ought. And because our actual practice of scientific inquiry is geared to such an idealized conception it transpires that current science as we actually have it both represents our best-achievable estimate of ideal science and moreover for this very reason constitutes our best-available surrogate for ideal science. Here as elsewhere we make the best that we can do in their direction serve us as functional surrogates for those inherently unattainable ideals.

CHAPTER SIX

IDEAL-SCIENCE REALISM

I. Reality is Adequately Described Only by Ideal Science, Which is Something We do not Have

Once we "distance" ourselves from the cognitive commitments of our science by recognizing that they can and frequently do go awry, we must also acknowledge that "our scientific picture" of reality is not fully accurate, admitting that we have neither the inclination nor the warrant for claiming that reality actually is as it is purported to be by the science of the day. As concerns our cognitive endeavors, "man proposes and nature disposes," and it does so in both senses of the term: it disposes over our current scientific view of reality and it will doubtless eventually dispose *of* it as well. Given this circumstance, we have little alternative but to presume reality to have a character regarding which we are only imperfectly informed by natural science.

Success in providing a definitive truth about nature's ways is doubtless a matter of intent rather than one of accomplishment. Correctness in the characterization of nature is achieved not by *our* science, but only by *perfected* or *ideal* science—only by that (ineradicably hypothetical) state of science in which the cognitive goals of the scientific enterprise are fully and reliably realized. We are constrained to acknowledge that it is not present science, nor even *future* or *ultimate* science, but only *ideal* science that correctly describes reality—an ideal science that we shall never in fact attain, since it exists only in utopia and not in this mundane dispensation. Scientific realism must thus come to terms with the realization that reality is depicted by *ideal* (or perfected or "completed") science, and not by the real science of the day, which, after all, is the only one we have actually got—now or ever. Our science is constituted of putative knowledge that does no more than to envision the truth as best we can discern it with the limited means at our disposal. Someone might object:

How can you maintain a clear line of distinction between real and
merely putative truth or knowledge in science? After all, might it
not possibly (perhaps even probably) happen that something that
is merely conjectured, suspected, or estimated to be true will actually turn out to be so?

The proper response is clearly: "Of course it can". But this is beside
the point. The distinction at issue is one that pertains not to the *content* of our claims, but to their *epistemic status*. Though it is possible
that we have hit upon the actual (definitive) truth, we clearly cannot
rely upon it. Even were it so, we could not *establish* it.

   We must maintain a certain tentative and provisional stance towards our own scientific "knowledge." We fully realize that what we
take to be true or real here is not always true or real. It is just this
consideration that constrains us to operate with the distinction between "our putative reality" and "reality as such." We realize that
what we think to be so—be it in science or in common life—
frequently just is not so. We certainly cannot identify our achieved
putative scientific truth with the real truth of the matter. No route save
idealization is able to effect a sure and general connection between
belief and the real truth. Only ideal or perfected science accurately
and correctly depicts reality, and not science as we actually have it
here and now. From the standpoint of epistemic status, truth is clearly
an idealization—not what we *do* (or ever *will*) *have*, but what we
could have if all the returns were in. It is thus in order to take a closer
look at this matter of cognitive idealization.

II. Scientific Truth as an Idealization

The history of science shows that our "discoveries" secured by way
of the inductive coherentism of the scientific method constantly require adjustment, correction, replacement. We cannot say that our
inductive inquiries about how things work in the world provide us
with the real (definitive) truth, but rather that they provide us with the
best estimate of the truth we can achieve in the circumstances to
hand. Only at the idealized level of perfected science could we count
on securing the real truth about the world that "corresponds to reality"
as the traditional phrase has it.

   The concept of science perfected—of an ideal and completed
science that captures "the real truth" of things and satisfies all of our
cognitive ideals (definitiveness, completeness, unity, consistency,
etc.)—is at best a useful fiction, a creature of the imagination and not
the secured Is, as its very name product of inquiring reason. This

"ideal science" I suggests, an idealization. We can only do the best we can in the cognitive state-of-the-art to *estimate* "the correct" answer to our scientific questions, which must suffice us because it is *all* that we can do. We recognize, or at any rate have little alternative but to suppose, that reality exists, accepting that there is such a thing as "the real truth" about the mind-independently real things of this world. But we are not in a position to state any final and definitive claims as to just exactly what it is like. Here we are confined to the level of plausible conjecture—of estimation.

Committed to the unproblematic claim *that* reality exists, we are, nevertheless, equally committed to the supposition that its nature is, in various not unimportant ways, different from what we think it to be. We can make no assured claims for our present-day science in this matter of "describing reality:" the most we can do is to see it as affording our very best estimate of nature's descriptive constitution. We realize that science as it stands does not give us "definitive knowledge." We know that we will eventually come to see with the wisdom of hindsight that each of the claims of current frontier science, taken literally in the fullness of current understandings and explanations, is strictly speaking false.[40] The realities of the situation force us to accept the presumptive falsity of the claims made at the scientific frontier of the present day.

Accordingly, we have no alternative but to presume that *our* science as it currently stands does not present the real truth. All we can and should say is that current science affords us the *best estimate* of nature's ways that we can make here and now. "Our truth" in matters of scientific theorizing is not—and may well never actually be—the real truth. However confidently science may affirm its conclusions, its declarations are effectively provisional and tentative, subject to revision and even to outright abandonment and replacement. We must presume that science cannot attain an omega-condition of final perfection. The prospect of fundamental changes lying just around the corner can never be eliminated finally and decisively.

Inductive inquiry is truth-estimation. And here, as elsewhere, the gap between the real and the ideal must be acknowledged. What inquiry provides is "our purported truth" as contradistinguishable from "the real truth itself." The idea of "the definitive truth" functions as a regulative conception for us. It characterizes what we ideally aim at rather than what we actually obtain; it guides the direction of inquiry rather than describing its achievements.

In scientific matters we are never in a position to claim definitive truth with dogmatic certainty. The most we can ever realistically do is to claim what we do have as being the very best that one can possibly obtain in the circumstances. Scientific progress is not of a character that encourages us to reify (hypostatize) the theory-objects of science *as presently conceived*—regardless of the date the calendar may show. Once we have taken a realistic look at the history of science, it is scarcely an appealing proposition to maintain that *our* science, as it stands here and now, depicts reality actually and correctly—at best one can say that it affords an *estimate* of it that will doubtless stand in need of eventual revision. Its creatures-of-theory may in the final analysis not be real at all in the form in which the theory envisions them. This feature of science must crucially constrain our attitude towards its deliverances.

One recent commentator maintains the view that science's aim regarding true theories "leads to the view that science represents a utopian, and therefore irrational activity whose *telos* is, to the best of our knowledge, forever beyond our grasp."[41] But this position is profoundly wrong. It fails to deal appropriately with the standard gap between aspiration and attainment. In the practical sphere—in craftsmanship, for example, or our health care—we may *strive* for perfection, but cannot ever claim to have *attained* it. And the situation of inquiry is exactly parallel with what we encounter in other domains—ethics specifically included. The value of a goal, even of one that is not realizable, lies not in the benefits of its attainment (obviously and *ex hypothesi*!), but in the benefits that accrue from its pursuit. The view that it is rational to pursue a goal only if we are in a position to achieve its attainment or approximation is a mistaken one. The goal can be perfectly valid, and entirely rational if the indirect benefits of its adoption and pursuit are sufficient—if in striving after it we realize relevant advantages to a substantial degree. An unattainable ideal can be enormously productive.

This is not, of course, any reason to abandon the link to truth at the purposive level of the aims, goals and aspirations of science. The pursuit of scientific truth, or for that matter any other ideal in life, is not vitiated by the consideration that its full realization is not achievable.

The idea of definitive finality in scientific inquiry is more than an idealization. The conception of capital-T for Truth thus serves a negative and fundamentally regulative role marking the fact that whatever we have actually attained falls short of realizing our cognitive aspirations. Definitive truth is not something available which we actually claim to have in hand, but marks a fundamental contrast that *regulates* how we do and must view our claims to have got at the truth of things. It plays a role somewhat reminiscent of the functionary who reminded the Roman emperor of his mortality, in admonishing us that our pretensions to truth are always vulnerable.

Ideal science is not something we have got in hand here and now. And it is emphatically not something towards which we are moving along the asymptotic and approximative lines envisioned by Charles Sanders Peirce.[42] For Peirce identifies ideal or perfected science with an ultimate condition of science that is "fated" to emerge in the eventual course of history. But there is, of course, no guarantee of this whatsoever. Perfected science is not "what will emerge when" but "what would emerge if"—where a lot of (realistically unachievable) conditions must be supplied. As far as the actual course of history goes, we must recognize that even if it made sense to contemplate the Peircean idea of an eventual completion of science, there would be no guarantee that this completed science (given it existed!) would satisfy the definitive requirements of *perfected* science. Peircean convergentism is geared to the supposition that ultimate science—the science of the very distant future—will somehow prove to be an ideal or perfected science freed from the sorts of imperfections that afflict its predecessors. But the potential gap that arises here can only be closed by metaphysical assumptions of a most problematic sort.[43]

Existing science does not and presumably never will embody to perfection cognitive ideals of definitiveness, completeness, unity, consistency, etc. These factors represent an aspiration rather than a coming reality: a *telos* or direction rather than a realizable condition of things. Accordingly, there is no warrant for identifying *ideal* or perfected science with *ultimate* science. Perfected science is not something that exists here and how, nor is it something that lies ahead at some eventual offing in the remote future. It is not a real thing to be met with in this world. It is an idealization that exists "outside time"—i.e., cannot attain actual existence at all. It lies outside history as a useful contrast-case that cannot be numbered among the achieved realities of this imperfect world.

III. Ideal-State Realism as the Only Viable Option

There is only one world in existence: the real world as it actually is. But we will not be able to say just what it is really like until the day when natural science has been completed and perfected, which is to say *never*. We must pursue the cognitive enterprise amid the harsh realities and complexities of an imperfect world. And this means that what we achieve in scientific inquiry is not the definitive truth as such, but only our best estimate of it. In forming a just appreciation of our scientific claims, the irremovable gap between the real and the ideal must once again be acknowledged.

The thesis that "science truly describes the real world" must be looked upon as a matter of intent rather than as an accomplished fact, of aspiration rather than achievement, of the ideal rather than tile real state of things. Scientific realism is *tenable* only when it is the *ideal* state of science that is at issue. (That, *ex hypothesi*, is what makes that state into an ideal one.) But ideal-state realism, while demonstrably correct, avails us less than we would like—we who occupy the sub-optimally real rather than the perfected ideal order of things.

It is ideal science alone that gets at the definitive truth of things to which authentic reality corresponds. Scientific realism is a viable position only with respect to that idealized science which, as we realize, we do not now have—regardless of the "now" at issue. The only sort of scientific realism that is unproblematically viable is an ideal-science realism. We cannot be unqualified scientific realists or rather, ironically, we can be so only in an idealistic manner, namely with respect to an "ideal science" that we can never actually claim to possess.

Perfected science is an idealization—as is the scientific realism that comes automatically in its wake. Now an ideal is not something we encounter in experience, but rather the hypothetical projection or extrapolation of what we encounter in experience. And the legitimacy of our cognitive ideals as regulators inheres in their *utility* as guides to inquiry, and specifically in their capacity to guide our thoughts and efforts in constructive and productive directions. It is a fallacy to see the validity of goals and ideals as residing solely in the presumed consequence of their *realization*. Their validation may reside not in arriving but in the benefits we realize in the course of the pursuit itself. The striving after an ideal science that affords us "the ultimate truth" about the workings of nature seems to be a *telos* of just this sort. (We arrive at the perhaps peculiar posture of an invocation of practical utility for the validation of an ideal.[44])

IV. Against Instrumentalism: The Descriptive Purport of Science

Should the mutability of natural science and the fact that our science, as it stands, cannot be claimed to depict reality correctly be taken to mean that science has the status of a merely practical device—an instrumentality for prediction and control devoid of any actually descriptive efficacy? Does natural science perhaps furnish no depiction of nature at all, but merely provide guidance to action? Such a stance is embodied in the traditional doctrine of instrumentalism, which takes roughly the following position:

Science has no descriptive or existential import at all. It is simply an instrumentality for calculating what observational consequences will ensue (or will probably ensue) if certain things are done (or left undone)—above all, what results will be obtained when certain measurements are taken. Its theories are "O more than devices for generating reliable predictions and guiding effective control. Thus science is a "black box," as it were, into Which we put some information (data or assumptions) in order to get out predictions about events or instructions for modes of intervention. But the propositions that figure in the contents of this black box must be construed as devoid of any descriptive content—any claims to characterizing the nature of the world. As an Instrumentality of prediction and control, science is wholly free of commitment that certain sorts of things really exist and actually have such-and-such a nature. The theories adopted by science are not to be construed as assertoric propositions. The question of the truth of theories or of the existence of the things they envision simply does not arise. Theories are mere rules for drawing inferences to actual or possible observations: successful and fruitful as guides to prediction and control. The theories of natural science thus do not deal with objectively real *things* and their *modus operandi* at all, but merely provide observation-coordinative *rules* which, being rules, may be more or less useful, but will not be true or false.

As the instrumentalist sees it, we must abandon the traditional view of science as a venture in securing information about the *modus operandi* of a nature that underlies observable phenomena and provides for them through causal mechanisms. Our scientific theories are no more than a practical device—a set of rules that facilitate effective interventions and verifiable predictions, mere tools for guiding future observational expectations in the light of past experience.[45] As one recent writer put it, to accept a scientific theory is not to accept it as *descriptively true*, but rather merely as *empirically adequate*; it is not to endorse the theory substantive declarations, but merely its observational predictions.[46]

Instrumentalism refuses to understand the theoretical claims of science at their descriptive face value, but insists on subjecting these claims to a reinterpretation that confines their bearing to the phenomenological/observational realm. It maintains that theorizing science should not be conceived as simply involved in the traditional venture of description, assertion-as-true, and causal explanation. Instrumentalism regards science as a strictly practical endeavor that does no more than guide our expectations and canalize our interventions in the world.

Kantian terminology is useful here. Kant distinguished between objective reality and objective *validity*, holding that space, for example, is not objectively *real* at all, but is objectively valid or "empirically real" in that we can relate it to the phenomenal objects of our experience. It must characterize all cognitively meaningful *phenomena* but has no self-subsisting *ontological* standing at all (CPuR, B44). Much the same sort of distinction is at issue in an instrumentalist view of the "laws of nature" in our scientific theories. In particular, the theoretical entities of scientific theorizing do not have a mind-independent ontological status—are not objectively "real things" at all (not *entia per se*). They only have an "empirical reality" in facilitating explanation, prediction, and control. Like the equator, they "lie in the eyes of the beholder" as serviceable fictional items devised by their users (they are *entia per aliud*). And to have a legitimate role in an appropriately devised cognitive framework is one thing; actually to exist is another. Never the twain need meet.

Accordingly, instrumentalism insists that it is necessary to reorient the goal structure of science away from its traditional teleology of answering our questions about the causal *modus operandi* of nature. The instrumentalist prohibits us from taking at face value those claims that natural science gears to unobservable entities. The whole issue of the descriptive truth of theories simply drops away at this level. Natural science becomes devoid of any *ontological* implications. It coordinates overt phenomena and does not trade in covert "realities." "Science without ontology" should be our maxim.[47] Instrumentalism is a sort of deconstructionism of natural science. (It tries to do for *theoretical* entities what Bertrand Russell tried to do for *fictional* entities—to reinterpret talk that is *ostensibly* about entities in terms that beat no ontological weight at all.)

The instrumentalist wants to "play safe" with respect to ontological commitment. Waving aloft the banner of William of Ockham, he does not want to multiply entities beyond absolute necessity, and so he strives to be rid of unobservable entities—electrons, genes, electromagnetic fields, and the like. In his view, those theoretical statements of science that purport to characterize the make-up of such unobservables have no real existential and descriptive import as such. For instrumentalists, talk about unobservables is simply an oblique way of describing the behavior of observables. Even as "the equator" is no more than a useful fiction that enables us to find our way about in the world, so those supposed "theoretical entities" of natural science are purely fictional devices that are useful for purposes of prediction and application. On this approach, science is not a description of reality but a useful fiction that produces results.

Such, then, is the position of instrumentalism. But why should one take this stance? For the issue we face is not: "Is instrumentalism a *possible* doctrine?" Rather, it is: "Is it an *attractive* position?" It is not the *availability* of the doctrine but its *appropriateness* that is in question. What can be said for instrumentalism in this regard?

The instrumentalist doctrine clearly has its problems. Our scientific theories can be viewed as constituting a contentless black box or a mere computing device that provides for calculations that mediate between observational data-inputs and observational data-outputs—a mere instrument of convenience devoid of any descriptive import. But this is hardly a satisfactory position if we take the traditional view of science as an instrumentality for answering our questions about the world.

After all, we want to know "What is really going on in the world?" The very reason for being of science is *information* about the "external world"—securing answers to our questions about how things stand in nature in terms of description, classification and explanation. Admittedly, in developing science, we are very much interested in mastery over phenomena through prediction and control, but that is only a part of it. The cognitive impetus of securing answers to our questions about the world is crucial. The object of the enterprise is to provide answers to our descriptive and explanatory questions about the things and processes of this world and their modes of operation. It should enable us to understand and predict the ways of trees and people and planets by allowing us to account for the behavior of things in causal terms, answering along the lines of *why* water freezes or barometers fall. And here instrumentalism leaves us wholly in the lurch.

V. Realism and the Aim of Science

The reason why *Homo sapiens* instituted the scientific enterprise in the first place was to secure information about how things work in the world. In the cognitive setting of the equation that defines the descent of a freely falling body ($s = 1/2\ gt^2$) there is an implicit group of explanatory stipulations of an emphatically existential and descriptive import.

—There is such a force as gravity deployed over a gravitational field engendered by material objects.

—This force is characterized by a constant quantity g specifying the "acceleration due to gravity".

And this situation is typical. The statements of natural science are generally made and received with descriptive and informative intent. An interpretative context of description links those equations of natural science with objective reality—at any rate as regards the matter of aim and aspiration. This is what the scientist (generally) hopes and strives for—and it is with the expectation of this goal that his statements are received by the laity. The prime aim and object of the scientific venture is to provide us with reliable and accurate descriptive information about the true make-up of a reality that is not of our making and where existence and nature are wholly independent of our cognitive endeavors.

Admittedly, the contentions of our science as they stand here and now may not be—nay presumably are not—actually adequate to reality itself. But we would abandon all descriptively informative aspirations if we failed to acknowledge their *purporting* (although perhaps failing) to depict matters as they stand in the real world. The intention to describe the world is a crucial aspect of the goal-structure of science—the very reason for the being of the venture (however far our actual performance may fall short of its realization). We introduce these "theoretical entities" in the first place in order to answer questions about the constitution and operation of the physical furnishings of nature.

A seemingly knock-down argument for scientific realism takes the following form:

(1) Whatever is a physical part of what exists itself exists.
(2) The world-as-a-whole (the physical universe) exists.
(3) Those theoretical entities of science (quarks, electrons, black holes, etc.) are constituent parts of the physical universe.
(4) Therefore, the theoretical entities of science actually exist.

But this argument is no better than a near miss because premiss (3) is not quite right as it stands. For this premiss to be tenable, the qualification "held to be" must be inserted: the theoretical entities of our science are only *held to be* parts of nature. But the argument does make transparently clear the realistic *purport* or intent of natural science. We develop the enterprise in order to give an account of what there is in the world.

From the very origin of natural science, it has been the aim of the enterprise to explain the obscure and unobservable in terms of that which we can investigate by the use of our senses.

> [The school of Aristotle] in discussing the origins of things and
> the constitution of the whole universe, established many facts not

only by plausible argumentation but even by the demonstrative
mathematical reasoning, and for the knowledge of matters beyond
the reach of observation (*ad rerum ocultarum cognitionem*) they
developed a good deal or material regarding matters that themselves can be investigated.[48]

The characterizing mandate of natural science is to furnish information about how things work in the world—about "what makes nature
tick." In abandoning realism we would turn our back on the definitive
descriptive and explanatory aims and tasks of the scientific enterprise.
In attempting answers to our questions about how things stand in the
world, science offers (or at any rate, both *endeavors* and *purports* to
offer) information about the world. The extent to which science suc-
ceeds in this mission is, of course, disputable. (And no doubt in this
discussion the issue of success in prediction and control will have to
play a central role.[49]) But this does not alter the fact that science both
endeavors and purports to provide realistically authentic descriptions
of what the world is actually like.

The theory of sub-atomic matter is unquestionably "a mere theory," but it could not help us to explain those all too real atomic ex-
plosions if it is not a theory about real substances. If I hypothesize a
robber to account for the missing jewelry, it is not a hypothetical robber that I envision but a perfectly real one. Similarly, if I theorize an
alpha particle to account for that photographic track, it is a perfectly
real physical item I hypothesize and not a hypothetical one. Only real
objects can produce real effects. There exist no "hypothetical" or
"theoretical entities" at all, only *entities*—and hypotheses and theories about them which may be right or wrong, well-founded or ill-
founded. To re-emphasize, the "theoretical entities" of science are
introduced not for their own interest but for a utilitarian mission, to
furnish the materials of causal explanation for the real comportment
of real things. And they cannot accomplish that job satisfactorily
without being seen as real objects that form part of the physical furnishings of the world. After all, we develop science in order to tell the
world's causal stories—to give a causal accounting for how it is that
the things that happen in the world happen. If we did not (think that
we) need those theoretical entities to tell that causal story, they would
not be there.

Science makes assertions all right, but *guarded* assertions. When
we look to *what* science declares, to the content and substance of its
declarations, we see that these declarations purport to describe the
world as it really is. Of course, when we look to *how* science makes
its declarations and note the tentativity and provisionality with which
they are offered and accepted, we recognize that this realism is of a

guarded sort that is not prepared to claim flatly that this is how matters actually stand in the real world. Despite a commitment to realism at the semantic level of assertion-content, there is no longer a commitment to realism at the epistemological level of assertoric commitment. Realism prevails with respect to the *language* of science (i.e. the content of its declarations) even after it is abandoned with respect to the *status* of science (i.e. the ultimate tenability or correctness of these assertions). Thus our inability to claim that natural science as we understand it depicts reality correctly must not be taken to mean that science is a merely practical device—a mere instrument for prediction and control that has no bearing on describing "the nature of things." What science says is descriptively committal in making claims regarding "the real world," but the tone of voice in which it proffers these claims always is (or should be) provisional and tentative.

An instrumentalist will, no doubt, try to make capital of the circumstance that the realist is not actually in a position to insist that those purportedly descriptive theories actually describe matters *correctly*. But here the realist has a convenient reply:

> So what else is new? Of course, those scientific theories I endorse are endorsed tentatively. I realize full well that they are no more than provisional estimates of the truth. But this is a matter not of their assertoric content (which is reality purporting), but of their epistemic status (which is tentative and defeasible). We must not confuse the *substance* of our assertions with their *evidential standing*.

We must, of course, recognize that there is a decisive difference between what science *accomplishes* and what it *endeavors* to do. And it is thus useful to draw a clear distinction between a *realism of intent* and a *realism of achievement*. Scientific realism skates along a thin border between patent falsity and triviality. Viewed as the doctrine that science *indeed describes* reality, it is doubtless untenable, but viewed as the doctrine that science *seeks to describe* reality, it is virtually a truism. We are certainly not in a position to claim that science as we have it achieves a characterization of reality. In *intent* or *aspiration*, however, science is unabashedly realistic: its *aim* is unquestionably to answer our questions about the world *correctly* and to describe the world "as it actually is" The "real truth"—authentic truth about reality—represents a conception to which we stand committed throughout the whole project of rational inquiry because truth affords its aim, though not its actual achievement. The orientation of science is factual and objective: in aim and aspiration it is concerned with establishing the *true* facts about the *real* world, however much it may fall short of attaining this goal.

The fact thus remains that its concern to resolve questions about the real world is the *raison d'etre* of the scientific project. Of course, we have no advance guarantee of success in this venture, and may well in the end have to recognize our limits and limitations in this regard. But this consideration affords no reason to abstain from doing the very best we can at providing full-fledged *descriptions* of the world. The theories of physics purport to describe the actual operation of real entities—those Nobel prizes awarded for discovering the electron, the neutron, the pi meson, the anti-proton, etc., were intended to recognize an enlargement of our understanding of nature, not to reward the contriving of plausible fictions or devising of clever ways for coordinating observations. However gravely science may fall short in performance, nevertheless in aspiration and endeavor it is unequivocally committed to the project of depicting "the real world," for in this way alone could it discharge its constituting mandate of answering our questions as to how things work in the world. The world-picture of natural science is—at best—a tentative or aspiring depiction of nature.

To accept scientific fallibilism does *not* mean that one must give up on the idea that scientific inquiry is a matter of the pursuit of truth regarding the workings of nature. Fallibilism simply means that we must make those descriptive and ontological claims of science in a somewhat tentative and provisional tone of voice. We must distinguish between the mission of the scientific project and its actual *achievement*. In intent, science unquestionably seeks to describe objective reality. But the circumstances in which we labor preclude our claiming that science actually achieves this aim. Yet while we must accept this fallibilistic view of science, the fact remains that the *aim* of getting at the truth about the world's ways represents the very essence of the enterprise.

Commitment to a realism of intent is inherent in science because of the genesis of its questions. The ultimate basis of the factually descriptive status of science lies in just this continuity of the issue of science with those of "prescientific" everyday life. We begin at the prescientific level of the archetypal realities of our prosaic everyday-life experience. The very reason for the being of our scientific paraphernalia is to resolve our questions about this real world of our everyday-life experience. Given that the teleology of the scientific enterprise roots in our commitment to the "real world" that provides the stage of our being and action, we are also committed *within its framework* to take the realistic view of its mechanisms.

Instrumentalism puts the cart before the horse. As far as the working scientist is concerned, scientific theories do not exist for the sake of prediction and control, but the other way round—prediction and control are of interest because they serve to monitor the adequacy of our theorizing about objective reality. Accommodation of the phenomena—"empirical adequacy" as it were—is *not* the be-all and end-all of scientific theorizing; it is merely a part of the test criteria for the adequacy of this theorizing.

Instrumentalism thus draws an incorrect conclusion from the undoubted fact of the fallibility and corrigibility of science.[50] This corrigibility does *not* mean that one should not make existential and descriptive claims about "the real world" in the context of science. It merely means that one must make them provisionally, talking in the hypothetical mode: "*If* 'our science' is correct, *then* electrons exist and have such-and-such features," etc. We must acknowledge that our science is ontologically committed in its descriptive and explanatory mission—in its intent or endeavor—though doubtless imperfect in its execution of this mandate.

VI. The Pursuit of Truth

Some theorists are tempted by the following sort of argumentation:

> Neither can we claim to have attained the definitive truth in scientific matters, nor can we even say that we are approaching it more and more closely. It follows then, that there simply is no such thing as "the real truth" in this domain. This whole absolutistic notion should simply be abandoned.

It must be said emphatically that the fallibilistic tenor of the present discussion does *not* underwrite such an all-out sceptical abandonment of "the pursuit of truth."

To be sure, some of the most prominent philosophers of science of the age have given up on truth. Rudolf Carnap teaches that theorizing science should never make flat assertions but only statements of probability.[51] Again, Karl Popper has argued long and hard that we must abstain from staking claims to truth in the sciences; that scientists should never *believe* the theses they devise but view them as mere conjectures, which they must try (and even hope) to falsify and must never regard as claims of substantive fact.[52] Thomas Kuhn's reading of the history of science leads him to reject any claim that science presents us with the truth of things.[53] Why, then, not accept this verdict and follow the sceptical path in dropping all reference to "the pursuit of truth" as regards the aim of science?

sceptical path in dropping all reference to "the pursuit of truth" as regards the aim of science?

The answer is straightforward. It is manifestly the *intent* of science to declare the real capital-T Truth about things. Without this commitment to the truth we would lose our hold on the teleology of the aims that define the very nature of the enterprise of inquiry. The characterizing *telos* of science, after all, is the discovery of facts—the providing of presumptively true answers to our questions about what goes on in the world and why things go on as they do. Resolving such issues calls for espousing—and rightly espousing—various theses about it. In holding that scientific inquiry yields information about the world, one is constrained to hold that it entitles us to *accept* certain factual theses—with "acceptance," of course, to be understood as at least a tentative endorsement of the truth. Any view of scientific claims as *information*-providing must proceed on an acceptance-model of rational inquiry into "the truth" of things. Our attempts at descriptive information may misfire; we may well, of course, not actually succeed in finding "the real truth." But unless we are prepared to take a committal stance towards what we do find—unless we are prepared (at least tentatively) to *claim* truth for our findings and so to accept them (at least provisionally) as asserting what is actually the case—we must simply abandon an information-oriented cognitive stance toward the world. (It would not make sense to think of scientific inquiry as a project in truth-estimation if there were no truth to be estimated.)

We have undoubtedly learned in the school of bitter experience that there is no alternative to presuming that our science as it currently stands does not achieve the definitive Truth. It is one thing to speak of "getting at the truth" in the language of aspiration and quite another to speak of it in the language of achievement. Truth *estimation* must be differentiated from truth *presentation*. The whole crucial contrast between the "real truths" of the perfected cognitive condition of things and merely purported or ostensible truths of the cognitive state-of-the-art would come apart if we abandoned our (regulative) commitment to the view that there is such a thing as the "real truth" and a mind-independent reality that determines it as such.[54] If science was not in its aim and aspiration an *attempt* to get at the real truth of things (an attempt that is, admittedly, imperfect and, as best we can tell, generally ends in failure), then the entire project of providing *information* about the world—of answering our questions about how things actually stand in extra-phenomenal nature—would become altogether unworkable. To abandon truth is to abandon the whole project of inquiry. A sceptical rejection of "the pursuit of truth" as a regulative ideal would abort the scientific project of rational inquiry into nature from the very outset.

Science does no more than endeavor to provide us with the very best answers currently available to our questions. The fact that these answers are probably incorrect and certainly incomplete is beside the point. The crux is that we have questions and want answers. The answers that science gives us are the best that can possibly be had at this time of day and thus represent the most that can currently be asked for. To abandon the whole information-seeking venture because much of the information it provides is misinformation would be to overreact. The sensible thing, in inquiry as elsewhere, is to do the best we can, and to settle for the best we can get. There is no reason why we should abandon scientific realism at the level of intent and aspiration.

In abandoning a dedication to the real truth, we would be reduced to talking only of what we *think* to be so. The contrast with "what actually is so"—the "real truth" of things—would no longer be available. We would now only be in a position to contrast our *putative* truths with those of others, but could no longer operate with the classical distinction between the putative and the actual, between what we think to be so and what actually is so. And at this point, the idea of *inquiry*—aimed as it is at increasing our grasp of the truth of things—would also be abandoned. It would be senseless to investigate something whose very existence is rejected, and to endeavor to estimate something that is not there—or at any rate presupposed or assumed or postulated to be there. In abandoning truth—in refraining from assuming or postulating that there is indeed such a thing as "the real truth of the matter" in regard to how things work in the world—we would no longer be able to conceptualize the project of scientific inquiry as we standardly do.

Such a substantiation of realism is, in effect, a transcendental argument for realism from the very possibility of science as it is standardly conceived. For given that science is by nature a project of explaining the world's occurrences—so that the very aim or aspiration of science involves a true characterization of nature's operations— one could straightforwardly say that a realism of sorts (i.e. a realism of aspiration) inheres in the very possibility of science. To be sure, "possibility of science" here means "possibility of fully achieving the aims of science" and not "possibility of securing the sort of science we actually have." Its thrust is aspirational rather than actualistic; it looks to truth attainment rather than to truth estimation. And so this sort of argument is not quite as powerful a defense of realism as is sometimes believed, seeing that the realism it secures is one of aspiration rather than one of achievement.[55]

CHAPTER SEVEN

IDEALIZATION AND IMPORTANCE IN SCIENCE

I. Why Importance Matters

Notwithstanding the infeasibility of perfecting science, the ideal of perfected science nevertheless plays an important part in our understanding of the scientific enterprise. What matters in scientific inquiry is progress, and this is determined not through the merely numerical proliferation of findings but through their size—not their mere numbers but the magnitude of their importance in the larger scheme of things. It is clear that without the distinction between the important and the unimportant at our disposal, mankind could neither adequately understand, successfully teach, or effectively practice science. Now perhaps the most critical fact about scientific importance is that it is an index of quality: of comparative significance in the context of understanding. Importance is thus a *comparative* conception: one thing is more important than another. Accordingly importance is an inherently elitist conception: there is nothing democratic about it. It is precisely because one finding is more important than another that it claims and deserves a larger amount of attention and respect. Importance in scientific discovery is thus a significant issue. And—as we shall see—idealization is a key factor here.

Note, to begin with, that importance in general is a *relational* conception that connects persons with purposes. Something is important *to* someone *for* something, even as eating a good diet is important to people-in-general *for* the maintenance of their health. Now what will concern us here is specifically cognitive and in particular scientific importance in the sense not of the importance *of* science for something else (such as human well being) but rather importance *in* science. What is at issue here is thus the importance *to* serious inquirers *for* the proper understanding of nature's ways.

People have little difficulty in telling us what is *important*, but saying what *importance* is is another matter. Importance is like pornography—we can generally spot it when we see it all right, it's the matter of adequate definitions and standards that is the difficulty. But let us see what can be done.

Given the inherent significance of the issue, it is surprising how little literature there is on the topic. Only in one philosophical handbook or encyclopedia have I been able to find has an entry under the heading of *importance*, namely the Spanish encyclopedia of Ferrater Mora. Its entry is brief and I cite it in full:

> *Importance*: see *relevance*.

Not very helpful! One of the few contemporary philosophers of science who has written about the topic is Larry Laudan in *Progress and Its Problems*.[56] He rightly observes that "The literature of the methodology of science offers us neither a taxonomy of its types of scientific problems, nor any acceptable method of grounding their relative importance." (p. 13). But his own discussion is better at diagnosis than therapy: it offers us various examples of important problems, but no effective criteria for what it is that constitutes this virtue. In essence, Laudan sees problems as important to the extent that currently fashionable theories disagree about them, but unfortunately this idea shipwrecks on the circumstance that theories can disagree about smaller issues as well as large ones. To see how scientific importance functions we will have to look in a different direction.

Perhaps the most basic consideration on the subject is that being cognitively important is something rather different from being interesting. For interest is something subjective, being dependent upon what it is that an individual happens to be interested in. Interest is person-relative—it is a matter of what someone happens to *find* interesting. Scientific importance, by contrast, is a matter of how prominent a role a fact or finding deserves and thereby demands in an adequate exposition of an area of inquiry. It accordingly does—or should—represent an objective issue.

So understood, the crux of scientific importance is the matter of understanding—of the negotiation between fact and mind. Cognitive importance is a concept that belongs not to abstract logic but to the domain of information management. The importance of a fact hinges on the following question: "How large a loss by way of emptiness or confusion would be created for our grasp of a certain domain if we lost our grip on the information at issue." Cognitive importance consists in making a difference for adequate understanding. It is a matter of how large a gap would be left in the body of our presumed knowledge by losing the item at issue.

But how are we to proceed in assessing the importance of scientific findings—and, above all—how might we be able to measure this?

To say that one fact or finding is more important than another within the problem-setting of a particular subject-matter domain is to make a judgment of worth or value. Accordingly, it merits a greater expenditure of intellectual resources—of attention, concern, time, and effort to discover, learn, explain, and teach the item at issue. Importance, that is to say, is a fundamentally economic concept—one of the pivotal concepts of the rational economy of cognition.

And so what we have to deal with here is an essentially seismological standard of importance. It is based on the question "If the concept or thesis at issue were abrogated or abandoned, how large would the ramifications and implications of this circumstance be? How extensive would be the shocks and tremors reverberating throughout the whole range of what we (presumably) know?"

Along such a line of thought, the "importance" of a factual issues will turn in the final analysis, on how substantial a revision in our body of scientific beliefs is wrought by our grappling with it, that is, the extent to which resolving the question at issue causes geological tremors reverberating across the cognitive landscape. But two very different sorts of things can be at issue here: either a mere *expansion* of our science by additions, or, more seriously, a *revision* of it that involves *replacing* some of its members and readjusting the remainder so as to restore overall consistency. This second sort of change in a body of knowledge, its *revision* rather than mere *augmentation*, is, in general, the more significant matter, and a question whose resolution forces revisions is likely to be of greater significance than one which merely fills in some part of the *terra incognita* of knowledge.

Importance accordingly is *a comparative concept of intellectual economy*: represents the extent to which one thing deserves more attention (time, effort, energy) than another. The crucial thing for importance is thus inherent in the question of *how much*—how prominent a place in the sun does a certain idea or concept deserve. This is best viewed *in the light of the idea of a perfected textbook for the domain at issue*. And importance will here be reflected in space-allocation. To reemphasize: the crucial determinative factor for increasing importance is the extent of seismic disturbance of the cognitive terrain. Would we have to abandon and/or rewrite the entire textbook, or a whole chapter, or a section, or a paragraph, or a sentence, or a mere footnote?

Scientific importance is therefore not a qualitative but a relational feature, a function of how one item (fact or idea etc.) relates to the others. It is a matter of discursive prominence, of space allocation in the context of systematization: When something is important here, then a lot else depends on its being the way it is.

II. The Quantification of Scientific Importance

Importance is bound to be reflected in how much occasion there is to have recourse to our idea on fact in the course of an adequate systematization of the domain at issue. This approach reflects a fundamentally pragmatic perspective. It views cognitive objects such as concepts, ideas, theories as being *tools*. And with any sort of production process—be it physical or cognitive—the importance of a tool lies in how much occasion one has to make use of it.

We thus arrive at what might be characterized as *the ideal space-allocation standard of importance*. A scientific idea, concept, principle, thesis, theory, finding, or fact is important exactly to the comparative extent to which merits space allocation in a perfected exposition of its field.

Since importance in such a sense—as already noted—is a fundamentally economic conception, it encounters the economically pivotal factor of limits or finitude. But now the crucial factor is not—as is perhaps more usual—that of absolute size but rather that of comparative size. It is a matter of deserving this-and-so much of the overall pie. And the cardinal principle in this regard is that no matter how large or small a pie is, there is only one of it to go around. All we can ever partition of anything is 100% of it: you can't get an increase on 100% and exactly 100% of anything is ever available for partition or allocation.

Now if one fact of finding deserves an additional one percent of the overall pie of attention, concern, etc. then that percent has to come away from something else. To assign more importance to something is to attribute less importance to another. This being so, it follows that since importance is a matter of percentage shares. We are playing a zero sum game in attributing importance.

Accordingly, one key mechanism for implementing the idea of importance lies in the general principle that the comparative size of an elite (at a certain level of eliteness) is given by a fixed relationship to the overall size of the group. This means that there will be a definite and perspicuous relation between the size of a population (P) and the size of an elite (E). To be sure, there are different possible approaches to characterizing the quantitative relationship obtaining between the size of a population and its elite. The two most familiar approaches here are, for one, the *exponential* ($E = \sqrt{P}$, called here are, for one, the *exponential* ($E = \sqrt{P}$, called Rousseau's Law—or in general $E = P^k$, with $0 < k < 1$). And the other major approach is the *proportional* ($E = \frac{1}{10} P$ or in general $E = k\%$ of P) or kP, with $0 < k < 1$. Our present approach is one that moves along the direction of the latter alternative. We will, however, take an iterative perspective here, taking the line that an nth-order elite is the elite existing within an $(n-1)$st order elite. As a result we have the situation of Display 1. What is at issue here is a kind of cognitive Richter Scale of importance based on the idea of successive orders of magnitude.

Display 1

A HIERARCHY OF ELITES

$E_1 = kP$ (with $0 < k < 1$)

$E_2 = k^2 P$

$E_n = k^n P$

III. Quality Distribution

To illustrate the just-indicated approach to cognitive importance, consider from the indicated perspective a more or less average scientific/technical book of monograph. Of such a treatise we can say that it is going to be divided into chapters, sections, paragraphs, and sentences. For the sake of discussion, we may suppose a situation that is roughly as per Display 2 (page 100). The result will be a more or less standard book of some $10^5 = 100,000$ words or 250 pages.

Display 2

A HYPOTHETICAL TREATISE

10 chapters per book

10 sentences per chapter

10 paragraphs per section

10 sections per paragraph

10 words per sentence

In terms of space allocation we have the situation of Display 3:

Display 3

SPACE ALLOCATION IN OUR HYPOTHETICAL TREATISE

1 book ~100%   (level 1)

1 chapter ~10%   (level 2)

1 section ~1%   (level 3)

1 paragraph ~0.1%   (level 4)

1 sentence ~0.01%   (level 5)

NOTE: In general, we have it that one level n unit merits a space allocation of $\sim \dfrac{1000\%}{10^n}$

If attention—and thus, effectively, space—is importance-reflective attention is—as per indeed aligned to importance (a big assumption, this, and one that is highly idealized) then we will have the upshot that our illustrative book will contain ideas or findings at the level of magnitude indicated in Display 4.

Display 4

QUALITY LEVELS

[1]   1 big (first importance) idea for the book-as-a-whole.

[2]   10 sizeable (second importance) ideas: one for each chapter.

[3]   100 moderately (third importance) ideas: one for each section.

[4]   1,000 smallish (fourth importance) ideas: one for each paragraph.

[5]   10,000 elemental (fifth importance) ideas: one for each sentence.

Building on this preceding illustration, let us follow through somewhat further on the above-mentioned idea that the quality-level of fact/findings can be measured in terms of their "magnitude" which is characterized as per Display 5 (page 102).[57] And, of course, our book analogy could be replicated on a larger scale in such a sequence as: cognitive domain, discipline, substantive, specialty, problem-area, problem, problem-component.

Display 5

A fact/finding in a given field has the quality magnitude	*If it deserves this percentage of our total attention/concern— that is, time and space— with this field*
1	100% (= 10^2)
2	10% (= 10^1)
3	1% (= 10^0)
4	0.1% (= 10^{-1})
n	10^{3-n}%

IV. Estimated vs. Actual and Real vs. Apparent

The presently contemplated approach to importance is thus comparatively straightforward, being predicated on the idea that the importance of an item within a given domain of deliberations is simply an index of the comparative amount of attention it deserves and thereby of the comparative amount of space that would be devoted to it in a fully adequate exposition of the domain at issue.

And this idea of domain-relative importance can be readily enlarged—at least in theory—by contemplating the idea of an idealized Perfected Scientific Library in which the totality of domains of deliberation would be comprehensively encompassed. In this idealized Perfected Scientific Library each domain of factual knowledge would be given its canonically definitive systematization—its perfected account in terms of correctness and completeness.

This model of a Perfected Library is—to be sure—something very different from the Borges Library contemplated by the Argentinean polymath Luis Borges. For the Borges Library is universal: it deals not only with actuality but seeks to map out the realm of possibility as well. Accordingly, the vast bulk of its holdings will be works of fiction rather than of science. Our Perfected Scientific Library, by contrast, concerns itself with fact alone, and leaves fiction aside.

Of course the constitution of even our more modest library involves a vast amount of idealization. This simply reflects the fact that it is real rather than putative importance that has been the focus of our concern. If we want to come down from the fanciful level of idealization that this involves, then we must deal with the reality of actual science libraries in place of that idealization. We must, in short, take the Hegelian line that the real is rational, and that the reality of things stands surety for that otherwise unattainable idealization.

For the *importance* of a question or answer that arises in one state-of-the-art state is something that can only be discovered with hindsight from the vantage point to which the attempts to grapple with it had led us. In science, apparently insignificant problems (the blue color of the sky, or the anomalous excess of background radiation) can acquire great importance once we have a state-of-the-art that makes them instances of important new effects that instantiate or indicate major theoretical innovations.

This being so, it should be clear that when we ourselves actually engage in the business of attributing importance to facts and findings we are providing *estimates* of importance. Importance for science as we have it here-and-now is one sort of thing—namely putative or estimated and thus subjective importance—while real, objective importance is a matter of how matters stand in ideal or perfected science.

The crucial fact is that progressiveness, insignificance, importance, interest, and the like will all have to be seen in practice as state-of-the-art relative conceptions. And in consequence, an item's cognitive importance must be taken to hinge on the question of how critical it is in securing an adequate understanding of the subject-matter domain at issue as this domain as it stands here and now. We are, in sum, constrained to proceeding at the level of estimation by letting apparent stand in for actual importance.

And it is just here that the element of idealization comes in. What actually is important is a matter of how things stand in a perfected or completed state of science. Real as opposed to putative importance involves the element of idealization. We can, of course, be mistaken on our judgments of importance. As emphasized above, the wisdom of eventual hindsight is going to have to come into it, so that in actual practice the issue is less one of determination than one of estimation.

The pivotal role of hindsight makes the fact that *apparent* importance—importance as we judge it here and now—is something rather different from *real* importance: that is, importance as it will eventually emerge with the progress of science. The nature of things is such that this difference can never be allowed to drop from sight.

For all practical purposes, then, it will not be "ideally deserved" space allocation that is our working index of importance but actual space allocations in the actually existing literature. We have no choice but to work with actual libraries rather than that hypothetical Perfected Library. And this has significant consequences.

V. The Role of Citation

For one thing, it means that in terms of availability our most practicable and available approach to importance is through citation studies. For now the comparative amount of space allocation—which we can estimate by the number and length of citations—will have to have our effective measure of importance. This idea can be vindicated as follows.

As concerns the distribution of items (findings) over quality levels we find the situation of Display 6 when we turn to articles in the scientific literature. A zillion studies of citation statistics confirm the dramatic picture of exponential decline obtains. And the lesson is clear: given the *modus operandi* of scientific discourse, importance can just as effectively be estimated in terms of prominence in citation space as by prominence in discussion space.[58] Given that *science-as-best-we-can-devise-it* is more or less by definition our best available *estimate* of *science as it would ideally be developed* the two can be viewed in practice as representing two sides of the same coin.

Display 6

THE CITATION DISTRIBUTION OF ARTICLES

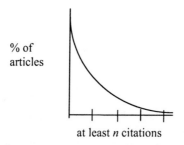

% of
articles

at least *n* citations

Another perspective on the issue is also instructive.

The etiquette governing the *modus operandi* of scientific publication has two critically important features in this regard: (1) it coordinates findings (ideas, principles, theories) with the names of their discoverers, and (2) it mandates giving people credit for findings that are relevant by way of evidentiation, presumption, or consequence. The mention of cognitively relevant findings is thus mirrored in the mention of names.

This means that short of using citation indices one can also proceed via the name indices of texts and handbooks to effect an estimate of importance. Such bibliographic aids afford an oblique approach to estimating the importance of findings. And, of course, no more than an estimate is at issue here. For it has to be acknowledged that in view of the ever moving boundary lines of the frontiers of knowledge and the shifting ebb and flow of fashions in matters of theorizing have the unavoidable consequence that importance as best we can judge it is not a fixity but an ongoingly varying parameter.

A good many well-recognized phenomena can be accounted for on this basis. For example, when there is a "reduction" between fields of investigation—when field *B* is "reduced" to field *A*—there will be a substantial accession of importance to *A*, since now all those *B* findings are absorbed by it. The new found relevancy of *B* issues to *A* issues means that all those reference to *B*'s finding and finders will become credited to *A*.

VI. A Dialectical Digression

At this point a brief digression into methodology is indicated. In clarifying the concept of scientific importance we confront three issues along the lines already noted, to wit:

- What does one *mean* in calling something an *X*.
- What sort of *authorizing evidence* will standardly entitle one to call something an *X*.
- What reason is there to think that the authorizing evidence at issue is adequate to the meaning at hand.

That is, we need to inquire about: (1) meaning or truth conditions, (2) evidentiation or use conditions, and (3) a rationale of adequation that coordinates the second to the first. Where does the issue of scientific importance stand in this regard?

The present chapter has sought to clarify both the *meaning* and the *use* of "scientific importance." On the side of meaning conditions we have seen that its crux is a matter of space allocation in *ideal* science. On the side of use conditions, by contrast, we have noted that since the realm of the ideal and perfected is inaccessible to us, the use-conditions pivot on the issue of space collection in actual (rather than ideal) science as best it can be assessed through citation indexes and other statistical bibliographic aids. And the conformity between the two is governed by the realization that actual science as we actually have it is our best available estimative surrogate for the ideal science as that we do not.

"Influential" certainty doesn't *mean* "important." But nevertheless being influential in our best-available *test* for importance in science. Turning blue litmus paper red is certainly not what we *mean* by "acid." But it is nonetheless a pretty good test of acidity. Of course what we need in such cases is a theory, an explanation, for why the test standard (be it litmus-change or influentiality) deserves to be seen as an indicator for the subject-item (acidity/importance). But can such an account be provided in the present case of influence and importance? The answer is clearly in the affirmative. For in the end, a thesis or theory just would not belong to actual science if it were not part of our best-available estimate of what belongs to ideal science.

This stance of seeing the actual as a surrogate for the ideal is of course of limited applicability. In fields other than science we cannot presume a correlation between attention and importance. Take philosophy and even the philosophy of science—indeed take as an instance this very issue we are considering, namely that of importance.

Surely this is a not unimportant topic—and yet as was noted at the very outset it is one that has attracted virtually no attention at all.

But back to the basics. In and of itself, scientific importance, like the idea of scientific truth on which it pivots, is predicated upon what is by its very nature a decidedly idealized conception. And in this imperfect mundane dispensation of ours we have no access to the ideal. And so, in matters of science too we have no alternative but to let the best estimate that we can get make do provisionally as a place-holder for the best there is. Fortunately, while actual importance in science looks to ideal conditions, *de facto* prominence as reflected in carefully designed citation analyses is able to provide an effective working surrogate for it.

CONCLUSION

The preceding deliberations have sought to show why and to illustrate how ideals function, both in general and now specifically in the cognitive domain. And it emerges that we employ the mechanisms of truth conditions and use conditions so as to allow manageable standards to provide working surrogates for unrealizable idealizations. For while idealized concepts afford a highly useful apparatus of linguistic communication, nevertheless to avail ourselves of this resource we must "compromise" and let suitably achievable surrogates do duty (in the mode of use-conditionality) for those unrealizable idealizations. To proceed in this way by means of "linguistic compromise" is not to betray our commitment to ideals but to do the best we can to put them to work amidst the harsh conditions of a difficult reality.

But why have recourse to such idealizations at all? Why employ a terminology whose assertoric meaning as reflected in truth conditions outruns its determinable basis for actual use? Why not make all those qualifications and approximations explicit?

The answer is straightforward. To do this would render the process of communication hopelessly cumbersome. If we could not speak of a "straight road" as such but had to speak of "a road that is relatively straight as roads go but exhibit such-and-such deviations," and similarly in every comparable situation, we would deprive ourselves of the prospects of efficient and effective communication. All these sorts of qualifications can be left unsaid as something that intelligent users of the language themselves supply spontaneously and tacitly as a part of their understanding of how language works.

So the interesting and in a way ironic fact of the matter is that the use of these idealization concepts finds its justification in pragmatic considerations. Those linguistic idealizations that figure prominently in our thought and discourse have an ultimately pragmatic rationale. For while such concepts as truth, importance, desirability, and justice wear their ideally on their sleeves their validity ultimately rest on practical considerations regarding their utility in reasoning and communication. We have recourse to them not out of an affinity for idealization as such but rather because this recourse to ideals proves itself to be eminently in the service of our practical objectives. For which ideas as such do not provide a template for the characterizing descriptions of the real they nevertheless do provide us with a basis for comparisons through which our descriptions of the real can be facilitated.

The present deliberations accordingly serve to indicate an ultimately pragmatic rationale for a communicative recourse to ideals, and thereby manifest the utility of idealizations as communicative instruments. For the salient lesson of the book is that "reality" of ideals lies not in their existential realization but in the positive results their utilization can enable us to achieve in practice. It is its functional efficacy rather than its actual realization as such that constitutes the reality of an ideal. Idealization, in sum, is a resource of significant utility for thought and communication. For ideals, unrealizable thought they be are an instrumentality of virtually indispensable value to a rational being that depends on conceptualized thought for the guidance of its actions in a world of vast and nearly intractable complexity. Idealization is a cognitive process whose utility for understanding and communication cannot be exaggerated.

To be sure, since ideals are as such unrealizable we must in matters of application have recourse to effectively realizable surrogates to stand in their place. But these surrogates would be impotent to do the work we ask of them if we failed to acknowledge their role as mere placefollowers for something grander and larger—an envisioned ideality towards which the mind's eye looks beyond the narrower horizons of experienced reality.

Plato was right in one regard and wrong in another. He was right to insist that we are amphibious beings who live in two realms, that of the mundanely real and that of the ideal. But he was wrong to insist that the latter is our true home with the former representing an exile into a realm of fraud and illusion. Platonic idealism involves a mistaken opposition to naturalism. Far wiser, surely, is a view that sees man as a creature that has come to be inserted (by whatever means) into nature whose own nature insists upon transcendence through the inherent tendency of his own characteristic resource—thought—to aspire to a standpoint that sees his presence in the world as endowed with purpose and meaning.

But what of the ontological status of ideals?

Some theoreticians have viewed ideals as actually existing things. Plato, for example, thought they existed in a realm of their own. He conceded that ideals are not part of the world's furniture, and that they are accessible through thought alone. But he nevertheless viewed them as being *found* rather than *made* by minds—as self-subsisting objects existing in a separate, world-detached domain of their own rather than as mere thought artifacts projected by the intelligences of this world. In this way, various theorists maintain the self-sufficient existence of ideals, independent of the sphere of mind. But such a "realistic" view of ideals has its difficulties. Once we abandon Plato's view that ideals are causally operative in the world directly and immediately, independently of their role in human thought, we lose the basis for assigning them a thought-independent existence. The "reality" of an ideal lies not in its substantive realization in some separate domain but in its formative impetus upon human thought and action in this imperfect world.

The object at issue with an ideal does not, and cannot, *exist* as such. What does, however, exist, is the *idea* of such an object. Existing, as it must, in thought alone (in the manner appropriate to ideas in general), it exerts a powerful organizing and motivating influence on our thinking, providing at once a standard of appraisal and a stimulus to action.

As Kant saw the matter, an ideal is "a *regulative principle* of reason" that directs our minds to look upon the world *as if* certain "idealized" conditions could be realized—conditions that, as we full well recognize, are not and indeed cannot be actual.[59] They exist not as such but only in idea or imagination. All our ideals are idealization imbued with an element of unrealism. The states of affairs they contemplate are mere fictions—mere thought pictures we cannot find actualized among the real furnishings of this world. The objects they envision do not and cannot exist as such; they are *putative* objects akin to merely hypothetical possibilities. Like the perfected state of utopian theorists or the wise man of Stoic philosophy, an ideal is destined to remain outside the realm of the world's realities. Ideals are best accommodated by an "idealism" that sees them as the products of mind (and mortal mind, at that).

The operation of ideals is accordingly confined to the domain of rational agents. Only mind-endowed intelligence can adopt guiding value ideals and act in their light with a view to approximating such essentially fictive states of affairs. (This shows that "idealism" in the present sense is also linked to a metaphysical idealism that sees mind as playing a key formative role in shaping the world's arrangements.)

With the eyes of the body we see thing as they are. With the mind's eye, we see them as they might and should be. (Imagination, that salient human resource, is crucial to the possession of ideals.) The discrepancy here can and should be not an occasion for discouragement but a goad to effort.

And so while ideals are never realizable as such, and always have an element of fiction about them, they are nevertheless indispensably useful for thought and communication. And in particular, in the cognitive sphere idealization they provide as with crucial instrumentalities in matters of the development and utilization of knowledge.

Notes

1. Rudolf Eisler, *Handwörterbuch der Philosophie*, rev. ed. by R. Mueller-Freinenfels (Berlin, 1922), entry "Ideals." For a useful general account see also the article "Ideale" by Rudolf Malter in Hermann Krings et al., eds., *Handbuch philosophischer Grundbegriffe* (Munich, 1973), 3: 701–8.

2. See Abraham Schlesinger, *Der Begriff des Ideals* (Leipzig, 1908), p. 1. Here, however, the name of this remarkable scientist and Leibniz-correspondent is misprinted as LARA.

3. Rudolf Eucken, *Geschichte der Philosophischen Terminologie* (Leipzig, 1879), p. 68.

4. In *Martianus Capella*, for example. See J. and W. Grimm, *Deutsches Wörterbuch* (1877), vol. 4, pt. 2, entry "Ideale."

5. See Rudolf Goclenius, *Lexicon Philosophicum* (Frankfurt, 1613), 1: 209.

6. Immanual Kant, *C.Pu.R.*, A568–B506, A578–B606.

7. Cicero, *De republica*, I, xviii, 28.

8. To be sure, inferential relationships obtain either way—there are both *truth* implications and *use* implications. The latter gives rise to what H. P. Grice called conversational implicatures. See his posthumous *Studies in the Ways of Words* (Cambridge, Mass.: Harvard University Press, 1989).

9. Cf. the author's *The Primacy of Practice* (Oxford: Basil Blackwell, 1973), pp. 107–23.

10. Some other issues relevant to the present deliberations are discussed in Chapter 1 (Meaning and Assertability) of the author's *Empirical Inquiry* (Totowa, N.J.: Rowman & Littlefield, 1982).

11. This chapter's discussion of truth vs. use conditions draws upon a paper published in *Logique et Analyse*, vol. 38 (1995), pp. 347–59.

12. While this account of communicative parallax is written with a view to *particulars* (such as the moon or the Great Pyramid), much of it will also hold, *mutates mutandis*, for diffused thing-kinds (water or copper) and thing-types (books or cows). What alone maters throughout is that there must be some objective item at the pre- or sub-theoretical level of which we can say that different accounts give different accounts of IT. (This is why the *lingua franca* of everyday life is critical.) The approach does not work for creatures-of-theory, however. We cannot say of Democritean atoms that Rutherford's theory is giving an alternative account *of them*. Creatures of theory cannot exist outside the confines of their particular theoretical habitat; sub theoretical things, however, can survive changes in the theoretical environment.

13. The point is Kantian in its orientation. Kant holds that we cannot experientially learn through our perceptions about the objectivity of outer things, because we can only recognize our perceptions as perceptions (i.e. representations of outer things) if these outer things are given as such from the first (rather than being learned or inferred). As Kant summarizes his "Refutation of Idealism":

Idealism assumed that the only immediate experience is inner experience, and that from it we can only *infer* outer things—and this, moreover, only in an untrustworthy manner . . . But on the above proof it has been shown that outer experience is really immediate . . . (*CPuR*, B276.)

14. The issues which this paragraph treats telegraphically are developed in more substantial detail in the author's *Induction* (Oxford, 1980).

15. The justification of such imputations is treated more fully in Chapter IX of the author's *Induction* (Oxford, 1980).

16. The justification of such imputations is treated more fully in Chapter IX of the author's *induction* (Oxford, 1980). Cf. also pp. 15–18 above.

17. Benedictus de Spinoza, *Ethics*, Bk. 1, axiom 6.

18. Compare the interesting paper by Michael E. Levin, "On Theory-Change and Meaning-Change" in *Philosophy of Science*, vol. 46 (1979), pp. 407–424.

19. Vagueness constitutes a context in which we trade off informativeness (precision) with probable correctness (security), with science moving toward the former, and everyday knowledge toward the latter. The relevant issues are considered in tantalizing brevity in Charles S. Peirce's short discussion of the logic of vagueness, which he laments as too much neglected, a situation that has since been corrected only partially.

20. Arthur Pap, *Elements of Analytic Philosophy* (New York, 1949), p. 356. Compare H. H. Joachim, *Logical Studies* (Oxford, 1948).

21. Cf. the author's *The Coherence Theory of Truth* (Oxford, 1973).

22. For the somewhat technical details of the argumentation that establishes this contention see Section III below.

23. Arthur Pap, *Elements of Analytic Philosophy* (New York, 1949), p. 356. Compare H. H. Joachim, *Logical Studies* (Oxford: Clarendon Press, 1948).

24. The definition vs. criterion dichotomy was the starting point of the author's *The Coherence Theory of Truth* (Oxford: Clarendon Press, 1973). It also provided the pivot for the critique of the coherentism of Blanshard's *The Nature of Thought* in his contribution to R.A. Schilpp (ed.), *The Philosophy of Brand Blanshard*, (LaSalle, Ill: Open Court Publishing Co., 1980). Several subsequent publications have kept the pot boiling, in particular Scott D. Palmer, "Blanshard, Rescher, and the Coherence Theory of Truth, *Idealistic Studies*, vol. 12 (1982): *Idealistic Studies* pp. 211–30, and Robert Tad Lehe, "Coherence: Criterion and Nature of Truth," vol. 13 (1983): pp. 177–89.

25. This is an issue on which I came to change my mind long ago largely owing to stimulating discussions held during the 1983–84 academic year with Professor Lorenz Bruno Puntel of the University of Munich.

26. Brand Blanshard, "Reply to Nicholas Rescher" in *op. cit.* pp. 589–600. (see p. 596.)

27. For a further development of these ideas, see the author's *The Coherence Theory of Truth* (Oxford, 1973) and *Cognitive Systematization* (Oxford, 1979).

28. Brand Blanshard, *The Nature of Thought*, 2 volumes, Allen & Unwin, London, 1939, vol. 2, pp. 267–68.

29. This essay is a revised version of a paper of the same title published in the *Review of Metaphysics*, vol. 38 (1985), pp. 795–806. In writing the paper I have profited by discussion with Dr. Geo Siegwart.

30. The author's *Cognitive Systematization* (Oxford: Blackwell, 1979) deals with these matters.

31. One possible misunderstanding must be blocked at this point. To learn about nature, we must interact with it. And so, to determine some feature of an object, we may have to make some impact upon it that would perturb its otherwise obtaining condition. (That indeterminacy principle of quantum theory affords a well-known reminder of this.) It should be clear that this matter of physical interaction for data acquisition is not contested in the ontological indifference thesis here at issue.

32. Note that this is independent of the question "Would we ever want to do so?" Do we ever want to answer all those predictive questions about ourselves and our environment, or are we more comfortable in the condition in which "ignorance is bliss"?

33. S. W. Hawkins, "Is the End in Sight for Theoretical Physics?" *Physics Bulletin*, vol. 32 (1981), pp. 15–17.

34. This sentiment was abroad among physicists of the *fin de siècle* era of 1890–1900. (See Lawrence Badash, "The Completeness of Nineteenth-Century Science," *Isis*, vol. 63 (1972), pp. 48–58.) and such sentiments are coming back into fashion today. See Richard Feynmann, *The Character of Physical Law* (Cambridge, Mass.: MIT Press, 1965), p. 172. See also Gunther Stent, *The Coming of the Golden Age* (Garden City, N.Y.: Natural History Press, 1969); and S. W. Hawkins, "Is the End in Sight for Theoretical Physics?" *Physics Bulletin*, vol. 32, 1981, pp. 15–17.

35. See Eber Jeffrey, "Nothing Left to Invent," *Journal of the Patent Office Society*, vol. 22 (July 1940), pp. 479–81.

36. For this inference could only be made if we could move from a thesis of the format $\sim(r)$ $(r \in S \, \& \, r \Rightarrow p)$ to one of the format (r) $(r \in S \, \& \, r \Rightarrow \sim p)$, where "$\Rightarrow$" represents a grounding relationship of "furnishing a good reason" and p is, in this case, the particular thesis "S will at some point require drastic revision." That is, the inference would go through only if the lack (in S) of a good reason for p were itself to assure the existence (in S) of a good reason for $\sim p$. But the transition to this conclusion from the given premise would go through only if the former, antecedent fact itself constituted such a good reason that is, only if we have $\sim(r)$ $(r \in S \, \& \, r \Rightarrow p) \Rightarrow \sim p$. Thus, the inference would go through only if, by the contraposition, $p \Rightarrow (r)$ $(r \in S \, \& \, r \Rightarrow p)$. This thesis claims that the very truth of p will itself be a good reason to hold that S affords a good reason for p—in sum, that S is complete.

37. Note however, that to say that some ideals can be legitimated by practical considerations is not to say that all ideals must be legimated in this way.

38. For an elaboration of this issue see the author's *Conceptual Idealism* (Oxford, 1973).

39. Cf. the author's *Peirce's Philosophy of Science* (Notre Dame and London, 1978).

40. This, in effect, is that salient insight of twentieth century philosophy of science from C. S. Peirce through K. R. Popper's *Logik der Forschung*, Vienna, 1939, to Nancy Cartwright's *How the Laws of Physics Lie* (Oxford, 1984).

41. Larry Laudan, "The Philosophy of Progress," (mimeographed pre-print, Pittsburgh, 1979), p. 4. Cf. *idem, Progress and it Problems* (Berkeley and Los Angeles, 1977).

42. Cf. the author's *Peirce's Philosophy of Science* (Notre Dame and London, 1978).

43. Peirce verges on seeing this point: but his latter-day congeners usually do not, and try to get by with wholly transcendental arguments from the possibility of science. CF. Wilfrid Sellars, *Science and Metaphysics: Variations on Kantian Themes (London, 1968)*.

44. To say that some ideals *can* be legitmated by practical considerations is not to say that all ideals *must* be legitmated in this way. On ideals and their ramifications see the author's *Ethical Idealism* (Berkeley and Los Angeles, 1986).

45. Instrumentalists purport to be driven to this position on grounds of a commitment to empiricism. But it is a strange sort of empircism they espouse. Traditionally, empiricism is the doctrine that all descriptive knowledge of the world must be grounded in experience. A doctrine which says that experience is impotent to provide for descriptive knowledge of the real (extraphenomenal) world is surely an anti-empiricist doctrine, not an empiricist one.

46. Cs. Bas van Fraassen, *The Scientific Image* (Oxford, 1980), pp. 46, 68–9, and *passim*.

47. We must even give up altogether on "physical objects." For physical object predicates cannot be introduced into a phenomenalist framework without resorting to gap-filling universals and counterfactuals in a way that is anathema to dedicated phenomenalists. Compare J. J. C. Smart, *Philosophy and Scientific Realism* (London, 1983), pp. 22–25.

48. Cicero, *De Finibus*, Book V, Chapter iv.

49. Compare the author's *Methodological Pragmatism* (Oxford, 1977).

50. Certainly, insturmentalists are often drawn to this position through positivist/empiricists sympathies, rather than fallibilist ones. But as the example of Hume already shows, the ultimate support of such a position itself generally lies in a scepticism based on historicist/relativist considerations.

51. See Rudolf Carnap, "The Aim of Indictive Logic," in *Logic, Methodology, and Philosophy of Science*, edited by E. Nagel, P. Suppes, and A. Torshin (Stanford, 1962), pp. 308–318.

52. Karl Popper, *logik der Forschung*, (Vienna, 1935).

53. Thomas Kahn, *the Structure of Scientific Revolutions* (University of Chicago Press, Chicago, 1970).

54. This discussion draws on Chapter XII, "Scientific Realism," of the author's *Empircal Inquiry* (Totowa, 1982).

55. Compare the criticism of Sellars given in footnote four to Chapter Three (see p. 158).

56. Larry Laudan, *Progress and its Problems* (Berkeley, Los Angeles, London: University of California Press, 1971).

57. An astronomical analogy is at work here, for the writer of n-th magnitude stars is also (roughly) proportional to 10^n.

58. The mapping of a citation space will of course, need to be done in a fairly sophisticated way. If X cites Y and Y cites Z, then X's thus oblique citation of Z should be allowed to redound to Z's credit.

59. Immanual Kant, *C.Pu.R.*, A569–B597.

BIBLIOGRAPHY

Badash, Lawrence, "The Completeness of Nineteenth-Century Science," *Isis*, vol. 63 (1972), pp. 48-58.

Blanshard, Brand, *The Nature of Thought*, 2 vols., (London: Allen & Unwin, 1939).

————, *The Nature of Thought* in R. A. Schilpp (ed.) *The Philosophy of Brand Blanshard* (LaSalle: Open Court Publishing Co., 1980).

————, "Reply to Nicholas Rescher," in R. A. Schilpp (ed.), *The Philosophy of Brand Blanshard* (La Salle, Ill.: Open Court, 1980), pp. 589-600.

Cartwright, Nancy, *How the Laws of Physics Lie* (Oxford: Clarendon Press, 1984.

Cicero, *De finibus*.

————, *De republica*.

Eisler, Rudolf, *Handwörterbuch der Philosophie*, ed. by R. Mueller-Freinenfels (Berlin: E. S. Mittler, 1922).

Eucken, Rudolf, *Geschichte der Philsophischen Terminologie* (Leipzig: Veit & Comp., 1879).

Feynmann, Richard, *The Character of Physical Law* (Cambridge, Mass.: MIT Press, 1965).

Fraassen, Bas van, *The Scientific Image* (Oxford: Clarendon Press, 1980).

Goclenius, Rudolf, *Lexicon Philosophicum* (Frankfurt, 1613). Reprinted Georg Olms, Hildesheim, 1964.

Grice, H. P., *Studies in the Ways of Words* (Cambridge, Mass.: Harvard University press, 1989).

Hawking, S. W., "Is the End in Sight for Theoretical Physics?," *Physics Bulletin*, vol. 32 (1981), pp. 15-17.

Jeffrey, Eber, "Nothing Left to Invent," *Journal of the Patent Office Society*, vol. 22 (1940), pp. 479-81.

Joachim, H. H., *Logical Studies* (Oxford: Clarendon Press, 1948).

Kahn, Thomas, *The Structure of Scientific Revolutions* (Chicago: University of Chicago Press, 1970).

Kant, Immanual, *Critique of Pure Reason*.

Laudan, Larry, *Progress and its Problems* (Berkeley, Los Angeles, London: University of California Press, 1971).

Lehe, Robert Tad, "Coherence: Criterion and Nature of Truth," *Idealistic Studies* vol. 13 (1983), pp. 177-189.

Levin, Michael E., "On Theory-Change and Meaning-Change," *Philosophy of Science*, vol. 46 (1979). Pp. 407-424.

Malter, Rudolf, "Ideal," in Hermann Krings (ed.), *Handbuch philosophischer Grundbegriffe* (Munich: Kösel-Verlag, 1973).

Palmer, Scott D., "Blanshard, Rescher, and the Coherence Theory of Truth," *Idealistic Studies*, vol. 12 (1982), pp. 211-230.

Pap, Arthur, *Elements of Analytic Philosophy* (New York: Macmillan Co., 1949).

Rescher, Nicholas, *Conceptual Idealism* (Oxford: Blackwell, 1973).

———, *The Coherence Theory of Truth* (Oxford: Clarendon Press, 1973).

———, *The Primacy of Practice* (Oxford: Basil Blackwell, 1973).

———, *Methodological Pragmatism* (Oxford: Blackwell, 1977).

———, *Peirce's Philosophy of Science* (Notre Dame and London: University of Notre Dame Press, 1978).

———, Nicholas, *Cognitive Systematization* (Oxford: Blackwell, 1979).

———, *Induction* (Pittsburgh: University of Pittsburgh Press, 1980).

———, *Empirical Inquiry* (Totowa, N.J.: Rowman & Littlefield, 1982).

———, "Scientific Truth as an Idealization," *Review of Metaphysics*, vol. 38 (1985), pp. 795-806.

———, *Ethical Idealism* (Berkeley and Los Angeles: University of California Press, c1987).

———, "_____" *Logique et Analyse*, vol. 38 (1995), pp. 347-59.

Schlesinger, Abraham, *Der Begriff des Ideals* (Leipzig: W. Engelmann,1908).

Sellars, Wilfrid, *Science and Metaphysics: Variations on Kantian Themes,* (London: Routledge & Kegan Paul, 1968).

Smart, J. J. C., *Philosophy and Scientific Realism* (London: Routledge & Kegan Paul, 1963).

Spinoza, Benedictus de, *Ethics*.

Stent, Gunther, *The Coming of the Golden Age* (Garden City, N.Y.: Natural History Press, 1969).

NAME INDEX

Albert the Great, 1
Anaximander, 36
Aristotle, 86

Badash, Lawrence, 115n.34
Becquerel, Henri, 61
Blanshard, Brand, 46, 54, 114n.24, 115n.26, 115n.28
Borges, Luis, 102
Bradley, F. H., 71

Carnap, Rudolf, 90, 116n.51
Cartwright, Nancy, 116n.40
Cicero, 2, 113n.7, 116n.48
Cromwell, Oliver, 2-3

Eisler, Rudolf, 1, 113n.1
Eucken, Rudolf, 113n.3

Feynmann, Richard, 115n.34
Fitche, J. G., 27

Goclenius, Rudolf, 113n.5
Grant, Ulysses S. , 8
Grice, H. P., 113n.8
Grimm, Jacob, 113n.4
Grimm, Wilhelm, 113n.4

Harvey, William, 61
Hawkins, S. W., 115n.33, 115n.34
Hegel, G. W. F., 64, 71

Hume, David, 116n.50
Husserl, Edmund, 61

Jeffrey, Eber, 115n.35
Joachim, H. H., 114n.20

Kant, Immanuel, 1, 4, 7, 23, 28, 63, 75, 84, 111, 113n.6, 113n.13, 117n59
Kuhn, Thomas, 90, 117n.53

Lana, Francesco, 1
Laudan, Larry, 96, 116n.40, 117n.56
Lehe, Robert Tad, 114n.23
Leibniz, G. W., 113n.2
Levin, Michael, E., 114n.18

Malter, Rudolf, 113n.1

Newton, Isaac, 68

Palmer, Scott D., 114n.23
Pap, Arthur, 114n.20, 114n.23
Peirce, Charles Sanders, 7, 69, 74, 81, 114n.19, 116n.40, 116n.43
Plato, 4, 6, 71, 110-11
Popper, Karl, 90, 116n.40, 116n.52
Puntel, Lorenz Bruno, 114n.25

Royce, Josiah, 71
Russell, Bertrand, 84